The Guide's Guide to Guiding

Garth Thompson

illustrations by Dov Fedler

JACANA

Dedication

I dedicate this book to Dave Rushworth, under whom I was apprenticed. I could never have wished to learn from a better naturalist. I have yet to meet anyone with so much time for his fellow man and understanding of all things wild.

First published by Russel Friedman Books cc in 2001
This third edition first published by Jacana Media (Pty) Ltd in 2006
Second impression 2010
Third impression 2011
Fourth and fifth impression 2012
Sixth impression 2013
Seventh impression 2014
Eighth impression 2015

10 Orange Street
Sunnyside
Auckland Park 2092
South Africa
(+27 11) 628-3200
www.jacana.co.za

ISBN 978-1-77009-247-1

Cover photograph by Dave Christianson, *Lions of Makalolo*
Printed by Mega Digital (Pty) Ltd, Cape Town
Job no. 002540

See a complete list of Jacana titles at www.jacana.co.za

Contents

Introduction

This book is a tribute to the guides of Africa, past, present and future. I trust that some of the lessons I have learnt over the years will be of benefit to you and that they will assist in giving the most important person to our industry, the tourist, a better safari experience. Without the tourist there would be very few national parks and safari companies. You and I would be employed in another profession. It is the tourists who come to us with their desires and expectations. Do we fulfil them?

I sadly confess that, in 26 years of active guiding, I have broken many rules in the 'principles of guiding', something of which I am not at all proud. As you read the words of this book, I trust that you will be able to learn from my mistakes and avoid having to follow the same path.

Guiding is much like politics and religion. There are basic principles, but many varied opinions and different viewpoints. I am sure that much could be added to this book with the input of many other learned guides. Indeed, some may not agree with all that I have written, but the object of this book is to present a few thoughts, ideas and lessons to those who are starting out in this exciting occupation.

May you enjoy this privileged profession as much as I have. I trust that you will reap the great rewards that it has to offer, in particular those of a closer understanding and connection with wildlife and nature, as well as peace of mind, camaraderie and fulfilment from sharing with our fellow man all that our incredible continent has to offer.

Garth Thompson
Harare 2006

Foreword

When I first met Garth in 1982, he was working at Hwange Safari Lodge as a professional guide. It was the first of what was to become my annual safari pilgrimage to Africa, leading groups from the Calgary Zoo travel program.

Garth was young, keen and energetic: he had all the necessary behavioural traits that would eventually lead to his remarkable success in his field. On that first trip to Zimbabwe, he represented my first contact with a full-time 'professional naturalist guide'. I must say, after enjoying a dozen Zimbabwe safaris utilizing Garth's professional guiding services, he has set a standard that I have used as a measuring stick for nature interpretation all over the world.

Not only is his plant and animal taxonomic knowledge extensive, but his comprehension of the ecological web and our place in it is profound. Knowledge, however, is a baseline tool that would serve no function had he not honed his own skills to transmit this information. And merely being a good storyteller is not enough, even with the appropriate knowledge base. Garth has a unique gift that has enabled him to weave his sensitivity of his clients' needs with the interpretive opportunities of a wilderness environment. He is continually questioning the complexity of the natural world around him, always challenging his own intellect and that of his peers and clients. Like a construction engineer, he builds upon this foundation of knowledge, and utilizes an almost poetic form of storytelling to share his understanding of the natural world with the people around him.

As a naturalist, he is ever keen and enquiring. As a storyteller, he is a master. As an advocate for the natural world, Planet Earth has no better friend. And now as an author, you have no better teacher. Drink in his words, as they are written by one who has lived by his convictions and beliefs, and by his own critical self-analysis. Without really knowing it, Garth has spent most of his life preparing to write this book. Those of us who have chosen our nature interpretation careers are incredibly fortunate that he has taken the time to share his hard-won experiences with us. We will all prosper professionally, and perhaps just as important, personally, from this creative masterpiece.

Brian Keating
Head of Conservation Outreach
Calgary Zoological Society, Canada

Acknowledgements

There are many people to whom I owe a great deal of thanks for their assistance in bringing this book to fruition.

First and foremost, I would like to thank Colin Bell and Haggis Black for their staunch support and persistent encouragement. Their belief in the book has enabled me to bring this project, about which I have talked for many years, to completion. Despite being two of the busiest people I know, they both tirelessly read, edited and advised on each chapter as they were slowly churned out.

Thanks to Haggis for his invaluable advice on medical matters. Both Haggis and Colin are enthusiastic and acclaimed photographers, and their input on photography is appreciated. Futher thanks to my father, Russell Thompson and Di Black for tirelessley reading and correcting the revised edition. Thanks to Mike Martin of Jacana Media for publishing and distributing the third edition, and to Dave Christianson for the use of his brilliant photograph which has been the cover to this book for the last two editions.

Special thanks go to my son David for his patient assistance in helping his computer illiterate father conquer the quirks and stresses that these frustrating machines seem to present at the most inopportune times. Thanks to Mel, my wife, and our children, for their understanding when I became a virtual recluse in order to finalise the book.

For reasons too numerous to mention, I would also like to thank the following people: Barney Besalink, Duncan Butchart, Sara and Steve Cameron, Sally Carney, Susie Cazenove, Nancy Cherry, Gary Clarke, Mari Dos Santos, Russel Friedman, Debbie Gardner, Liberty Henwick, Map Ives, Dee and Brian Keating, Chris Kruger, Henrietta Loyd, Mark Nolting, Michael Poliza, Chris Roche, Paul Schamberger, Susie Strange, Jan Teede, Keith Vincent, Dave Waddy, Arnie Wallace and Brian Worsley.

My special thanks to Dov Fedler, the cartoonist, with whom I spent happy days filled with laughter as he created pertinent illustrations.

Most of all, I wish to thank my clients, many of whom are now close friends. They have made my work so varied and interesting by accompanying me on wide-ranging and exciting adventures. Together, we have watched, experienced, appreciated and shared many windows of Africa's infinite beauty. Without these special people, none of the valuable lessons I have learnt would have been possible.

It is thanks to the precious time and convictions of all of the above friends that we have **The Guide's Guide to Guiding**.

Preamble

Ever since I can remember, I wanted to be a game ranger. Not an uncommon desire among the young boys I grew up alongside in what was then Rhodesia. We yearned to swop our confined, concrete classroom for the freedom and adventure of the 'Bush University'!

Each year at school when Careers Day came around, I would stand and stare for long periods at the display behind the desk on the Department of National Parks stand. These black and white photos portrayed a band of dedicated men, chasing giraffe across open plains in open short-wheel-base Land Rovers, with the intent to capture and translocate, firing a tranquillizing dart into the rounded rump of a white rhino, teaching wildlife conservation to groups of eager children out in the wild, capturing poachers bent on pillaging our country's national treasures, collecting snares that would inflict pain and suffering on innocent animals, resulting in a torturous death. I collected every pamphlet, brochure and roneoed sheet available. I took them home and consumed each word with hungry enthusiasm and youthful fantasy!

My brothers and I were very fortunate in that our parents took us camping in the various unspoilt national parks that graced so much of our country. These adventures and the invaluable exposure occurred during most school holidays and over long weekends.

I never realized that my guiding career really started at a young age. I had a yearning desire to explore any new area, wild or tame. I would then share the most scenic parts with family and friends. Growing up in the outer suburbs of what is now Harare, I discovered many little patches of wilderness. When my parents had friends around for afternoon tea over weekends, I was often called upon to take their guests to these various wild places.

So began a lifetime of guiding people from all corners of the earth. When I had finished my army service, my life-long dream came true: I was employed as the assistant wildlife manager at a lodge adjoining Hwange National Park. The lodge was situated within 30 000 hectares of private reserve bordering the national park.

In 1980, when Zimbabwe attained its independence, the tourist industry was reborn. I was extremely fortunate to be apprenticed to one of the best naturalists

Africa has ever produced. As good a naturalist as he was, he was even more in tune with people. Dave Rushworth had been in the Department of National Parks since 1962. He had been a ranger and warden in many of the country's national parks. His knowledge on all aspects of nature was phenomenal. He imparted this knowledge to all, in a patient, kind and dedicated manner.

Dave Rushworth had absolutely no need for money. He was oblivious to time and did not succumb to stress or pressure. He was equally at home with the rich, the poor, old and young alike. He treated all as equals and gave 110 per cent of himself to everyone, all of the time! From Dave I was fortunate to learn about many aspects of wildlife, but most of all, how to give our guests what they had come on safari for: a genuine wildlife experience, and to really feel wanted.

I worked for and learnt from this good man for three years. Dave then departed to manage a park for the king of Swaziland. I was left to step into his huge shoes. A few years later my wife and I were offered a partnership in one of the safari camps bordering Mana Pools National Park in the Zambezi Valley. During the years that we managed our new camp we also started up a small tour operation to facilitate our bookings. This was to grow and develop into a company arranging itineraries to many of the lodges, camps and safari operations around Zimbabwe and the neighbouring countries. At this time we started our own canoeing and walking safaris through Mana Pools National Park, a park in which I have had the privilege of sharing incredible scenery and concentrated wildlife with many people of all ages, from many walks of life, nationalities and social standing.

As tour operators we would annually visit nearly every camp and lodge in Zimbabwe, as well as a number of camps in Botswana, Zambia and Namibia.

During the last 26 years I have been fortunate to work as a guide in most parks within Zimbabwe, the Okavango Delta in Botswana, the Skeleton Coast and Etosha National parks of Namibia, the Luangwa Valley and Zambezi National Park in Zambia, the Serengeti, Ngorongoro Crater, the Selous and the Mahale Chimpanzee Park in Tanzania, as well as Zanzibar with its cultural history, combined with diving among its rich and diverse underwater gardens. I have climbed to the summit of Africa's highest mountain, Kilimanjaro, seen the game-rich parks of Kenya and been as far afield as the Volcanoes National Park in Rwanda, home to the rare and endangered mountain gorilla.

These are some of Africa's crown jewels that, since my childhood fantasy, have enriched me, not to mention the numerous life-long friends that I have made while sharing these spectacles. Strong bonds and relationships are forged by time spent together in the wild.

As a *guide* I have been afforded the opportunity of giving slide shows and wildlife lectures to many groups of people in North America, Europe, the Far

East, Australasia and Africa. These audiences have varied from three year olds in nursery schools to Prince Philip in Buckingham Palace.

It has indeed been a privilege to be a guide in Africa. I sincerely hope that those of us who are involved in this profession appreciate how fortunate we are to be paid to experience and share with our fellow men - who come from so many different parts of the world, have varied cultures, and are interesting and diverse personalities - all that Africa has to offer.

To those of you who have dreamed and fantasised about becoming a *guide*, to show and share the unlimited wonders that our great continent has to offer, I can assure you, it is all possible. You need only the desire to work with people for many hours of your waking day, a positive attitude, an enquiring mind and a genuine love and appreciation for all things wild. One small word of advice: never lose sight of the real reason you are there.

'So that's a guide?'

Chapter 1

What is Guiding all About?

Driving good-looking people around in an open safari vehicle, in your sleeveless khaki shirt, showing off your muscular sun drenched arms and impressing your guests on how close you can get to lions on a kill? Telling hunting stories around the campfire each night after your sixth Scotch? If that is your idea of guiding, not only have you purchased the wrong book, you are also in the wrong profession!

Guiding is essentially about a genuine enjoyment of people and an honest appreciation of, and dedication to, the many faces nature has to offer. It is indeed a privileged occupation. Imagine being paid to take people out into the wilds of Africa, every morning, afternoon and evening. To sit around the warm, flickering flames of a campfire each evening, savouring the rich smell of wood smoke, while friendships are formed and forged. The people for whom you are interpreting Africa have worked long and hard for months, even years, to come and see what you have to show them in a couple of weeks. They have great expectations of this brief interval of time.

You hold in your hands the opportunity to realise their dreams and fantasies of Africa - or to destroy them. It all depends on one *little* thing that in fact should play the *biggest* part in life: Your *attitude*. It's not their attitude that is relevant - they are paying you for a service and they are on a well-earned holiday.

*'Attitude is a **little** thing which gives you **big** results'*

What is Each Client's History?

Do you know or care? I was very fortunate to learn my greatest lesson in guiding in my third year as a guide. In 1983 a group of sixteen enthusiastic Texans from the Fort Worth Zoo spent four days on safari with us in Hwange National Park before moving on to a number of other parks around Zimbabwe. The group was as mixed and varied as you would expect any group of that size to be. Old and young, fat and thin, loud and quiet - you can imagine how many diverse personalities were present.

A few months later I went on my first visit to that amazing country, the United States of America. My young eyes were out on stalks for the entire duration of the visit. I went to Fort Worth to give a slide show at the zoo. The following night the group of sixteen safari 'alumni' got together at someone's home, each person bringing along their ten best slides from their recent African safari. As all relived their various experiences, I marvelled at the delight and joy they showed as each slide came up. It was enthralling to see, some months after I had been with them on safari, how much it had meant to them. I asked myself, had I really pulled out all the stops? I thought I had given of my best, but, what if I hadn't? Could I have done more to give these appreciative people a better wildlife experience?

After the slide show we stood around chatting and eating. I began talking to a girl called Becky, a quiet and unobtrusive soul, plump and in her mid-thirties, the type of person who doesn't expect the level of attention that an extrovert, blonde bombshell would. I asked her the standard run-of-the-mill question; 'So, when are you coming back to Africa?' I was expecting the standard reply of 'Oh, I just can't wait!' But Becky replied sadly, 'Never.' I was quite shocked at this unusual reply, and asked her why. She went on to tell me that both she and her husband had saved up for *five* years to send *her* to Africa! It had been her childhood dream to visit the great game reserves of Africa. I asked, with a little trepidation, how she had enjoyed her once-in-a-lifetime experience. She said it was better than she had ever imagined…

How many people like Becky go through our hands without us knowing the background to their visit? Imagine a sulky, arrogant, bored Romeo, rally driver of a guide, showering his attention on the good-looking blonde in the seat next to him, while ignoring his duty to show and share the countless wonders that Africa has to offer to the Beckys in the back of the vehicle?

More Food for Thought

Some years ago I was having lunch with friends who had been on a number of canoeing and walking safaris with our company. We were discussing how expensive safaris had become. Charles said they had planned to buy and install a satellite dish and decoder that year, but had decided instead to use the money to come on yet another canoe trip, from which they believed their two daughters would receive a richer experience.

On the way home I thought to myself, 'Here is a family that would rather spend their savings on canoeing with us for five days, than buy a satellite system that would give them more than a hundred different TV channels, and would last them for many years!' It made me realize what value, importance and priority a wildlife experience holds for people. Imagine giving them a mediocre safari!

In the mid-1980s a radiologist sold her deep freeze to pay for staying at our safari camp in the Zambezi Valley. I only found this out some time later and once again felt so privileged to be able to share all that a safari can offer with someone who had made such a personal sacrifice. Little did we know at the time that she would eventually give up her career as a radiologist and come to work in tourism as a travel consultant. Thanks to her enthusiasm and dedication to wildlife, combined with an understanding of a client's desires and aspirations, she eventually ended up as the managing director of a highly successful tour operator. Today, she is a prominent personality in the tourist industry of southern and central Africa. How much the travel industry owes to that deep freeze!

Wildlife Junkies

Over the years we have come to know a number of interesting characters who can ill afford a safari to Africa, yet they save up for two to three years to come out for their wildlife 'fix'. For some it is the most important event in their lives. Back in the large cities from which they hail, whenever the opportunity arises, they talk, dream, read and watch Africa on video and TV.

Do we as guides realize the importance and responsibility of our work? Do we take what we do for granted? Are we as enthusiastic as we were when we struggled to land our first job in the tourist industry?

Create the Magic

As guides, we hold in our hands the opportunity to make or break the dreams and fantasies that people have of Africa.

For many, some of the first words they uttered in life were 'jumbo', 'hippo' and 'zebra'. As children, they grew up on books depicting the

'Safari Junkie'

animals of Africa. During the 50s and 60s they were exposed to Tarzan films and the Daktari series. In recent times, the public has enjoyed well-produced wildlife documentaries that have taken years to film by patient and dedicated photographers and naturalists. They have read famous and romantic novels set in Africa and listened to the colourful and enthusiastic stories of friends and colleagues who have just returned from an African safari. Visitors to Africa certainly have high

'Create the magic'

expectations; but don't we all have high expectations of our hard-earned holidays? Look at all the promises in the glossy brochures, which lure visitors to our exciting continent. As a guide, the onus is now on you to create the magic.

What is Guiding all About?

Guiding is far more about people than animals. You may spend ten hours a day looking at four-legged animals, but you will spend between fifteen and eighteen hours daily with the two-legged ones. There are very few professions where you spend so much time with the same people. On a canoeing, walking or mobile camping safari, you are with your clients every waking hour, which is normally from dawn till around ten at night. Most of these safaris are five days or longer. During this time you are their guide, teacher, protector, friend, doctor, storyteller, cook and dish-washer.

I am often asked, 'You must hate taking out all those foreigners and being with people for so much of the time?' But look at it another way. As a guide you see the best side of humanity. Firstly, you work in the biggest and most beautiful office in the world. Secondly, your clients are on holiday. They are out for a good time. They want fun, laughter and safe adventure. They are also on foreign turf. That aggressive chief executive from Manhattan is out of his depth - he hasn't a clue how to track a rhino, or where to try and find your resident leopard. People who have high-ranking positions in society are often feared or idolised by the minions around them. In a wilderness situation, however, their platinum credit card can't protect them from a charging lion. That's why they hired you.

In modern society, people are worried about image, their looks, brand of clothes, jewelry, how they present themselves, what car they drive, where they live, what schools their children go to, which ski resort they frequent, which cocktail party is the right one to be seen at, with whom not to be associated. Yet, when these same people are out on safari, they drop all the social barriers and pretences they need to survive in *their* jungle. They meet other guests in the various safari camps who come from totally different social, financial, political and cultural backgrounds. Life-long friendships are often formed.

What draws these social opposites together? The answer lies in the beauty and

'Platinum credit card'

'Your theatre'

simplicity of untouched nature. If you had a little hand in it, too, imagine how rewarding it would feel.

When about to take some high-ranking businessmen out on safari in the past, I had been forewarned by their staff that I would be in for a hard time, because of their reputation for being fussy, aggressive, sullen, impatient, restless and difficult to please. But once the 'ogres' arrived, they turned out to be quite the opposite. When invited to visit them back in their ivory towers, eyebrows were raised by the staff, as the top executive gave an ecstatic welcome to a khaki-clad, rankless imposter!

Guiding is such a privileged profession: your 'office' is a massive park, teeming with so many colourful and interesting forms of wildlife. In turn, your park is a theatre, an amazing open air amphitheatre, where the props are real living trees, clouds, rivers and mountains. The orchestra comprises the combined melody made up from the sounds of the wind, bird song, gurgling rivers, a lion's roar, a hippo's snort, the eerie yodel of a black backed jackal. The animals are the actors, their beauty and actions speaking their parts. You are the presenter, with endless opportunities to share an ever-changing and unwritten show with your fellow man. Your guests from all corners of the globe and from all walks of life, are the mobile audience.

What Have They Come To See?

My family and I had never skied until the year of writing this book. What did we want out of a skiing holiday? Simple: lots of snow to ski on! We weren't too worried about the accommodation or standard of food. They would be added bonuses if the skiing was good.

Most people on a once-in-a-lifetime holiday to Africa want to be able to go back and say they saw a lot of game, mostly big! Birds, plants, insects, exclusivity, etc. are an added bonus. This raw fact may not fit into your perception of what you have to offer the clients with your immense bush knowledge.

'They came to see'

Sadly, it is a fact that applies to most first-time visitors.

Many visitors who have the money and desire to come back to Africa a second time will then be interested and specialise in the smaller animals, birds and plants, but they will still enjoy watching a big bull elephant stand on its hind legs to reach up into the browse line of an acacia tree, or a herd of five hundred buffalo in an extended line, their beady, bloodshot eyes peering over wet black noses at the intrusion to their daily grazing. No matter how many times one has been to Africa, who doesn't still enjoy the thrill of a lion kill, the squabbling growls erupting from around the carcass, the smell of an opened gut, the bloodstained faces of scruffy cubs?

If we had gone skiing and there was not enough snow to ski on, but had a brilliant ski instructor who explained to us how the Alps were formed, what their geological make up was, educated us on all the different pines and firs, took us to the best restaurants in the village, related the long and interesting history of the village, we would have made a friend and may have been impressed at his wide knowledge and enthusiasm for his job, *but* we would not have fulfilled our yearning desire to ski. When we returned home and all our friends enquired how our skiing holiday went, we would have said, 'Well, we met a very knowledgeable ski instructor who taught us so much; he was such a nice guy'. 'But did you ski?', would be the constant question. 'No, not really, there was hardly any snow to ski on,' would be the deflated reply! Remember that visitors come to Africa for maximum wildlife experiences. If they didn't, they would visit the safari parks in their own countries.

The 'Walking Encyclopedia'

Try not to impress your clients with how 'extremely knowledgeable' you are without showing them the 'snow,' about which they have fantasised and dreamed during the months prior to leaving for this game-rich continent. Leak out your knowledge at the appropriate times in the right quantities. The guests want to 'ski' on maximum 'snow' for as long as physically possible. They hunger to see more and more game. While you may have become bored with seeing your millionth impala, they may have never laid eyes on such a graceful creature, whose lithe body with its acrobatic leaps represents the ballerina of the bush.

So try to and look at everything through the eyes of a keen and enthusiastic first-timer.

'Everything is a once-in-a-lifetime experience'

'Walking encyclopedia'

Stop and spend at least ten minutes with their first impala herd. After your eager passengers have fired off half a roll of film on these perfectly formed animals, their index fingers will have stopped twitching and they will have calmed down and become receptive as you point out the difference in the sexes and the scent glands on the hind legs. You can then explain in simple English about their breeding, rutting, extended gestation and foetus retention in times of drought, feeding habits, rumination, great leaping abilities, etc. Only half of what you say will be retained, but it is relaxing for your guests to sit and watch and appreciate the animal while you unobtrusively educate them on what will later become a 'common' animal.

Never tire of spending time with any animal, no matter how common it may be or how many times your guests have visited Africa. These Africa 'junkies' come back time and again for their African 'fix' because the first time you took them on safari you 'spent time' slowly introducing them to all the members and secrets of the animal community in your park or country. Through this slow and gentle introduction using the correct blend of information, sightings and excitement, you will have them hooked on the earth's most incredible addiction.

Recently, I was a guest on a safari into the Okavango Delta. Some of the members in our group had never been to Africa before. Imagine their eager expectations of what they might see as we entered the Moremi Game Reserve, an animal warehouse filled with such a variety of different species of mammals, birds and trees. We arrived at our camp after dark on the first evening. Early the next morning we set off with our guide, whom we hoped would show us the exciting wares that this massive wildlife shop window had to offer.

Our guide was a young zoology graduate from Oxford University. As we drove from camp, we stopped every hundred metres so that he could point out various animals' footprints, dung, and birds. He described the full life-cycle and habits of various insects and spiders. He gave us a botany lesson on some of the interesting trees, grasses and aquatic plants. After about two hours we encountered our first mammals, a small herd of red lechwe. They were on the opposite side of a big lagoon, about 200 metres from the vehicle. After briefly watching them we turned around and headed back to camp for breakfast, arriving at around 09:30.

After breakfast, we showered and read and relaxed until lunch, after which it was suggested that we have a little rest and meet at the mess tent for tea and cakes at 15:30, followed by an afternoon game drive at 16:00.

At 16:20, after sitting around sipping tea and wasting good light and game viewing time, we left camp. We were all champing at the bit to get out and find some animals.

A few hundred metres down the road we left the vehicle and walked over to a baobab tree for an interesting 15-minute lecture on this amazing botanical landmark. Then we drove another two kilometres, rounded a small scrubby acacia tree, and there, set up beside a large lagoon was a drinks table, with all the imaginable beverages displayed on it, a silver ice bucket, crystal glasses, etc. There was a small campfire burning, surrounded by a ring of canvas chairs. It was still about 45 minutes before sunset.

Our charming guide offered us drinks and then produced a large map of the Okavango Delta and its surrounding area. He glanced at his assistant guide and said, 'Where shall we start? Ten thousand or one hundred thousand years ago?' For the remainder of the afternoon we were given the most detailed lecture on how the Okavango Delta was formed. When it was dark we had another drink and drove back to camp with the spotlight on, all of us desperately hoping we would see more than just the baboons we had disturbed when we walked up to the baobab tree earlier on. We were fortunate in seeing the small resident herd of impala that lived close to camp.

Although our guide had impressed us with the great extent of **his** knowledge, we, the guests, clients, tourists, wildlife enthusiasts, photographers, call us what you like, had only seen a herd of lechwe from a distance, a frightened troop of baboons and a family of impala illuminated by the spotlight, **all day!** Surely we could have had the lecture on the geological history of the delta while we lounged around camp from 09:30 till 16:20? It was our first day of game viewing and everyone was yearning to see a variety of interesting and exciting animals. Think about the Australians in our group who had never been to Africa before, and how much they wanted to see an elephant, buffalo or lion.

All the interesting lectures on spiders, plants and insects should have been reserved for later on the seven-day safari, after satisfying the desire to see the masses of mammals that live in Moremi Game Reserve. Afternoon safari activities can be so productive for game sightings; the light is perfect for photography. We were all anticipating an active afternoon's game drive.

In the fast moving society of the First World, people have very little time to relax and enjoy their environment. Time is extremely precious to people, so don't waste it trying to impress someone with how knowledgeable *you* are! Imagine your first days skiing, how keen you would be to get out there and give it a go. How would you feel if your ski instructor spent the whole day giving you lectures on the geological formation of the Alps? Your guests have come for the 'snow'. Let them ski!

How Much Does a Day Cost?

Have you ever thought about what goes into the cost of a day on safari?

Before we get into the 'all-inclusive' daily rate of the safari operation that you represent, or the airfare and air charters to get to your park, let's look at the personal sacrifice that most guests make before going on a safari holiday.

Most First World countries offer between two and five weeks' leave per annum to their hard-working citizens. Americans are rarely given more than two weeks' leave per year, and in a number of executive positions it is frowned upon to take both weeks consecutively.

To be as unbiased as possible, the following equation is formulated for a client earning *four weeks'* leave a year:

- Lets say that the average safari client earns the equivalent of US$5 000 a month.
- Of the 12 months during each year, he or she works for 11 months to earn one month's leave.
- Let us presume that person works a 5-day week.
- He or she therefore works for 220 days of the 11 months. This represents 20 working days each month. Earning $5 000 per month divided by 20 working days equates to a daily income of $250.
- Our visitors have worked long and stressful days to earn their leave. From the above example it is easy to ascertain that they have *worked 11 days* to earn *1 day's* leave.
- If they earn $250 per day and have worked for 11 days to receive one well-earned day's leave, this precious day is equal to $2 750!

The point I am trying to make is that if you waste a day's safari or part thereof because you were disinterested, burnt out, or disorganized; if you didn't take your radio when you left camp on your game drive; if you forgot to check your vehicle and all its equipment, and you had a flat tyre and no wheel spanner with which to change it, or you ran out of fuel, took a risk and got horribly stuck, (the list is endless), you would have cost your guests part of a day of a holiday they worked long and hard to earn.

On top of the $2 750 per day, we have not even taken into account the daily cost of staying in your camp. Let's say the average daily rate of an African safari camp is $325 per person per day. Don't forget the additional costs such as air fares, travel insurance, safari clothes, equipment, film, house and pet minders, many hours spent researching the safari, surfing the net, speaking to tour operators, reading books and watching videos on Africa and its wealth of flora and fauna.

Every visitor to Africa is going to place a different value on the daily cost of his or her safari. Even if you were to refund them all the money lost from a bad day, you could never refund the loss in terms of eagerness, anticipation and time for each safari outing. The measure of disappointment is incalculable, while the time lost is priceless and irreplaceable.

Most people are easy going and understanding when things don't go according to plan. However there are many unplanned events that Africa can throw at you from every conceivable angle. Try your level best to ensure that the cause of the wasted time and opportunity was not because of your negligence. Try to realize all the dreams and desires of the visitors with the incredible things our continent has available.

'Sorry no wheel spanner'

'Who pays your salary?'

Chapter 2

Tourism

'Live to observe, not be observed'

What Is a Tourist?

Never forget that tourists are the lifeblood of our industry. They are flesh-and-blood human beings, with feelings and emotions like our own. They have desires, dreams and expectations. Some fly halfway across the world and bring us their wants; it is up to us to make these happen. They are **not** just 'another FT', (sadly a derogatory word used in the tourist industry, the T standing for tourist and the F is left to your imagination) or 'Punter'. You don't work in a casino, far from it, so respect these people who come to you for a wildlife experience.

- They are the **sole** purpose of your employment.
- They **pay** your salary.
- Their tourist dollar provides the motivation for our African governments to protect large tracts of wilderness from an ever-increasing and land-hungry population. It creates huge employment for the surrounding community.
- The tourist dollar also ensures the protection of the multitudes of animals with which we so enjoy spending our time.

'The tourist dollar'

- The tourist dollar helps import the fuel that runs your safari vehicle, the tyres on which you drive, and the computers that run your reservation system.
- The tourist dollar assists in running the whole economy of your country.

'Tourist disciple'

In addition, tourists return to their countries with a belief in our wildlife sanctuaries and become dedicated disciples for the conservation and preservation of these sanctuaries. Through their enthusiastic stories to family, friends and work associates, they advertise your safaris and your country.

Many people come out as mere names on the arrivals list, but some become life-long friends. How good to know that you can win firm friends from such a beautiful and exciting workplace. Tourists give *you* the opportunity to go out and enjoy the bush and its contents each day, month, and most of the year.

We don't need any more reasons to realise the importance these people play in conservation and tourism. And, from our viewpoint as guides, in our families' future and survival.

Who Makes up the Tourist Industry?

You have chosen to be part of one of the most exciting industries in the world, the 'leisure industry'. Sure, there are long and awkward hours, you often are at work by dawn and continue till late each night. Over weekends and public holidays you are at your busiest. During these long hours you have the opportunity to see and learn so much. You will meet and interact with interesting and diverse individuals from a great variety of nationalities.

The leisure industry can be likened to a big wheel. The many types of employment that form the *spokes* of the tourist industry are all there to service the *hub*, which is the *'tourist'*, without whom there would be no wheel.

The spokes consist of hoteliers, guides, chefs, waiters, couriers, travel consultants, room cleaners, gardeners, croupiers, pilots, drivers, accountants, receptionists, telephone operators, laundry cleaners, advertisers, marketing and sales personnel, musicians, dancers, child-minders, kayakers, rafting oarsmen, photographers, boat drivers, bungee jumpers, rock climbers, mountaineers, canoeists, cyclists, riding instructors, grooms, ski instructors, parachute instructors, naturalists, computer geeks, bureau de change bankers, curio shop attendants, doctors, hunters, taxidermists, parking attendants, car cleaners, scuba instructors, deck-chair attendants, mechanics, plumbers, electricians, builders, life-savers, security personnel, air traffic controllers, flight attendants, game rangers and wardens, car hire, ski hire and bike hire agents, and so the list continues.

By reading this book, you are obviously involved or at least are interested in the 'guiding spoke' of the tourism wheel. Certainly, I believe one of the most interesting, exciting, challenging and rewarding of all the spokes!

Types of Guide

Guiding attracts a diverse and interesting group of people, who can be fitted into different categories.

The Macho Guide

These guides join the profession with a preconceived image. Sadly, wildlife guides are often compared with Italian skiing instructors or well-tanned and muscled life-savers! This image has been well earned by a large number of guides and hunters, many of whom appreciate the beauty of their clients more than that of the wildlife they are employed to present.

Who has not encountered the guide with the sleeveless khaki shirt open to expose a hairy, well muscled chest on which hangs a lion-claw necklace attached to a leather thong? Over one broad shoulder rests a heavy-calibre rifle, almost an extension to the body. A Swiss army knife, buck knife and long bowie knife adorn a bullet-laden leather belt supporting a pair of khaki shorts, one size too small! From these short shorts extend a pair of powerful legs that reach down to character-filled veldskoens. The right arm casually holding the shouldered rifle is home to at least five big elephant-hair bracelets, while its opposite twin is enveloped in a cluster of copper bangles, colouring the forearm with a dull, greenish hue. A cloth bandanna acts as a turban, holding in the thick black curls tied back in a tight bun behind a noble head, while a subtle earring glints in the African sun. Unfortunately, the piercing eyes are hidden by wrap-around dark glasses.

This is the image that many youngsters have of a 'professional guide'. What a great job to show people lion, elephant and buffalo, and save and protect them from these highly dangerous animals. Cock your rifle and hold it at the ready when the big bull elephant shakes his head and stares over his shining tusks at your cowering clients! That night while seated around the campfire, they will praise you for having saved them from a life-threatening situation, and will ply you with copious drinks and 'more' in thanks for your heroic services!

This kind of guide will often say how much he *loves the bush,* can never go to town, can't cross the street because there are too many cars and people. Yet follow him on his time off and you will see him happily sauntering down the city's main street with a Walkman blasting out the latest hit, full volume into his earphones as he heads towards his favourite pub.

'Macho guide'

Such guides never last long in the industry. They soon become bored with the outdoor life, the sun, dust and the same old boring animals. They grow tired of acting 'nanny' to a bunch of decrepit elderly tourists. Life wasn't as they expected it to be in tourism: those damned lions that everyone nags to see were far harder to find than expected; the last few close shaves with those old, retired 'bush generals,' the lone male buffalo were enough to spoil anyone's breakfast.

Eventually, they miss the trappings of city life, the local sports club and drinking buddies. Most of the people they have had to take on safari were from the 'blue-rinse brigade', - inquisitive old widows who were happily spending their inheritances.

One of the most important principles in guiding is:

'Live to Observe, not be Observed!

Be modest, honest and motivated in all that you do.

Parrot Guide

These guides learn most of what they know from books, not through time spent observing in the field. Alternatively, they will repeat word for word what they may have learnt from other guides.

They will stop at a baobab tree and reel off, in parrot fashion, all the scientific information that they memorised from the tree book.

While watching a herd of wildebeest, they will recite the exact number of days of the gestation period, the animal's height at the shoulder in centimetres, its weight down to the last kilogramme. These facts will be reeled off in a dull monotone, without feeling or enthusiasm.

Such guides can also fall into a category called the *'Wind-up Guide'* – someone who resembles a toy with a wind-up key in its back. These guides become wound up before leaving on a game drive. They then beetle down the same pattern of roads, stopping at the same

'Wind-up parrot guide'

tree, beehive, bird's nest, termite mound and old lion kill and give the same spiel at each place of interest. Clients soon realize they are with someone like a bus driver who has driven the same route for the past twenty years. But they were expecting a keen naturalist dedicated to the wild haven he is so fortunate to live and work in, bursting with energy and enthusiasm to show and interpret the fascinating creatures that inhabit his or her place of work. For many guides, English is not their mother tongue. In their defence it is difficult to master and feel comfortable with an unfamiliar language. Don't be quick to categorise them into the above category.

'You were born an original, don't die a copy'

Your guests want more than they can read from a book, television documentary or a computer. They will soak up the first-hand information that you obtained through your own personal observations. Don't forget that the only way to accumulate these is by spending *maximum* time in the field, with all your senses wide open to everything that is going on around you.

The 'Big 5' Guide

This guide prides himself in finding the 'Big 5' on every drive. These wildlife sightings are achieved by listening to the radio and pestering all the other safari vehicles as to what they have seen. This guide then zooms from one of the 'Big 5' sightings to the next, driving like a rally driver between sightings, and missing the essence of all that the African wilderness has to offer. Viewing their guests as 'checklist-ticking tourists,' they career around a natural area as if it was a theme park, bouncing from one good ride to the next. Naturally, everyone who comes out on safari would like to see the animals that make up the 'Big 5', but try to achieve this with creativity, sensitivity, understanding and appreciation for all that is around you.

'The big five drive'

'The Seloser Scout'

Escapist Guide

Guiding attracts a number of lost souls, some with drinking problems, broken marriages, or those who can't hold down a job for long. They are often full of hard-luck stories. They seek a job in the bush to get away from all their responsibilities and failures. After their sixth drink around the campfire, they attempt to obtain respect and sympathy for their plight and bore the client with their mournful stories of having twice been a millionaire, a hero from some forgotten war or a kind and loving father, whose wife ran off with his best friend and the children. This type of guide tends to drift from camp to camp, as his real worth becomes known.

Genuine Bush Lover, but Anti People

There are a number of guides who really enjoy all that the wilderness has to offer. They are often exceptionally knowledgeable in certain fields, on plants, birds, butterflies, etc. They are at their happiest when walking for days on end alone in the bush, being at one with nature, living simply, with time of no importance, and pursuing their special interests.

These guides are often former national park wardens, rangers, research officers or museum curators, who have spent most of their working lives dedicated to the protection and research of an ecosystem where tourists are *not* on the indigenous species list!

They were often very poorly paid in these government jobs and couldn't afford to educate their children. Many left the Department of National Parks because of government bureaucracy, corruption, or politics. Many begrudgingly join the commercial wildlife sector as guides or hunters. It enables them to continue a life in the bush, which has always been their place of employment, often even since leaving school. Most genuinely love and appreciate the outdoor life. Putting up with tourists is often the price they have to pay.

If such a guide meets a client who shares the same interest, be it birds or plants,

'The anti tourist'

he or she will excel as a guide, so pleased to find someone who appreciates the smaller things in the bush instead of hankering after big game. Such a person will often end up giving this type of tourist the trip of a lifetime.

Unfortunately, the 'average' tourist wants a maximum wildlife experience in minimum time, so there are not many folk who find a place on his checklist of enlightened people. This type of guide will therefore give a mediocre safari to the 'average' client. They will not go out of their way to try and satisfy the client's wants and desires. They will give just enough to ensure the client returns from the safari without a complaint, but will not form firm friendships or be requested as a guide again. Often, when asking clients a few weeks later who their guide was at a particular safari camp, they will struggle to recall his or her name and describe him as the 'plant person', or the guy who studied vultures for 25 years, or the woman who used to be the curator of the insect department in the Bulawayo museum.

How would you feel as a guide, if your clients couldn't remember your name a week after you had taken them on safari? Did you give them the best of your knowledge, show them your area and its contents to the best of your ability, or did you just drive around pointing out the obvious?

Prima Donna Guide

This is often the worst type of guide with which a poor, unsuspecting tourist can be lumbered! They are often burnt-out, opinionated, 'has been' guides, who were once sought after in their heyday by return clients or possibly by the rich and famous.

They may have become well known in guiding circles owing to a number of factors. They were possibly authorities in a particular field, be it ornithology, wildlife art, photography, journalism, elephant studies, lion research, great white hunters, etc. They may have then turned to guiding because of personal circumstances. Their name could have been made by guiding royalty, well-known movie stars, possibly billionaires - all those who rank highly in social circles.

'Prima donna guide'

Because of the celebrity status they may have come to enjoy, some become self-opinionated and will bore countless guests around the campfire each night with 'has been' stories of 'when I guided the Queen, Rockefeller, Elizabeth Taylor, or when I studied the White Lions of the Timbavati, shot the man eaters of Buggamazoo, saved all the animals in Operation Noah', and so on. There have been a number of such guides whose pinnacle in life has been an event in the past. If lumbered with what they perceive to be a 'common tourist' this type of guide can often be temperamental, unaccommodating, rude, sullen, aggressive, single-minded and generally unpleasant. Guests are then far better off with the lowliest apprentice guide in camp, who might not know a great deal, but is bright-eyed and bushy-tailed and tries continually to please.

> *I once asked a 'celebrity guide' who had hired me to give his young new guides a training course, why he didn't teach them himself? He replied 'I have not spent a life time of learning the secrets of the wilds to now feed it out as strawberries to swine!'*

These 'Prima Donna guides' often find it 'below them' to pour tea for their clients, load the cooler box, clean out their safari vehicle or do a number of other so-called menial chores. At the dining table they seek out the company of those whom they perceive to command the highest social rank. Because of their aloof and curt behaviour, they can destroy a safari for some average soul who has come to Africa for a special experience.

Should you be fortunate to make a name in guiding, never forget your modest beginnings or those 'common' clients that assisted you in getting there. Continue to share all that you have been privileged to learn with all and sundry. Don't forget, their money is the same. Often the 'average' tourist will give back so much in excitement and thrill at what you have shown them. Prima donnas don't belong to a world of nature and simplicity.

People's Person

These guides join the tourist industry because they genuinely enjoy the company of their fellow man. They are often very gregarious and have good communication skills and relaxed personalities, all of which assist in relating to the people they will meet from all walks of life.

Contrary to the reclusive animal lover, for this type of guide wildlife is a means to be with people. They learn enough to get by on a safari activity and keep their clients happy with stories and light hearted jokes. They do not delve too deeply into nature and will seldom have an in-depth knowledge of plants, grasses, stars, insects etc. Despite this, their easygoing, willing-to-please personality will often ensure that clients arrive back from a game activity satisfied. For the average tourist (which possibly accounts for 80 per cent of clients who go on safari) this is an ideal guide. The safari is productive and lighthearted and the clients do not have the whole encyclopedia of wildlife thrown at them in the first hour.

This type of guide is often quite relaxed and does not succumb to unnecessary pressure (always to have to race around to find lion, etc.) They therefore guide slowly and abide by their instincts, which normally produces good results in wildlife sightings. They are responsive to people's feelings, needs and desires; their relationship does not end when the guest climbs out of the safari vehicle on returning to camp. You will often see this type of guide sitting at the breakfast, lunch and dinner table chatting to a few guests long after the other guides have scuttled off to get some respite from people.

'People's person'

This type of guide likes to spend time chatting about all aspects of life. They show a genuine interest in where the guests are from, in their culture, work and family. They can converse on a large variety of topics, ranging from wildlife to sport, current affairs, travel and entertainment. They are not necessarily totally dedicated to the wildlife cause and they are as at home in the bush as they are in a city. They often look forward to their time off, away from wildlife, so they can pursue their other cultural and social interests.

This type of guide does not necessarily satisfy the avid birder, botanist or entomologist who are in single-minded pursuit of as much exposure to and information on their 'pet' subject as possible. For most tourists, however, a people-orientated guide will show them enough wildlife, make them laugh, feel at home, form lifelong friendships and give them a good time.

The 'average' tourists want to be satisfied that they have seen and photographed what they imagined they would experience. They like to feel wanted and not be treated like 'average' tourists. Their desire is to make friends with their guide, to have an uncomplicated stay and to leave happy, healthy and safe. This type of guide can make it happen.

'Superguide'

People and Wildlife Enthusiast

These are the best guides in the profession. They have a true love, appreciation and understanding for all things wild, with equal attention paid to the two-legged animals who have saved up and paid for someone to show, share and interpret this gift to them.

These guides have all the qualities of the people-orientated guide, but combined with those of the true bush lover and naturalist. At the top of the guiding pyramid, they are few in number and high in demand. Possibly the best indicator of the success and abilities of these guides is the number of clients who return and seek out their services, often booking him or her as an exclusive guide for the duration of the entire safari. These safaris may cover a variety of parks and wild areas in a number of countries, where species and habitat differ considerably. This type of guide often has the skills to guide on foot, by vehicle, canoe, boat, kayak, raft, mountain bike, on horseback or underwater - among the diverse life of a coral reef.

They have an in-depth knowledge of mammals, rock art, birds, plants, African history and culture, conservation issues, geology, reptiles, fish, insects and astronomy, apart from human skills. They make life-long friends with most of their clients through this common bond of nature's uncomplicated and diverse beauty, enhanced by unorchestrated experiences.

They are proud of their profession and take it seriously. It is often a lifetime occupation. They raise, educate and house their families from their vocation. Their families share the friendships with people from all corners of the earth.

Extraordinary Guides – Eccentrics

I have watched with interest this type of guide, who has the bemused clients spellbound by his antics. There is only a handful of these colourful characters, who often have very strong personalities, are great raconteurs and tremendous showmen without trying to be. Most have a very specialised 'pet subject', let's call it *'birds'*. They have the knack of turning their group into keen birders even if they arrived on the safari without the slightest interest in birds.

They are oblivious to time and, believing that everyone else is also totally absorbed by birds, they feel no pressure to find big game. The clients, who have now become spectators, are enthralled by the antics of this character, from whose hand they feed while the eccentric pursues his or her passion. Whenever an interesting bird is spotted, the vehicle is switched off, the bird patiently studied through well-used binoculars, often accompanied by mumbling noises equal to that of a mad professor, while notes are scribbled into a well-fingered bird or note book.

When such guides encounter a rare bird, they verge on becoming apoplectic in their behavior and will drive the vehicle through the virgin bush in pursuit of the bird, while the bemused clients hold on for dear life uttering shrieks of delight, as they are bounced from termite hill to antbear hole.

Very few guides can naturally pull off this kind of behavior. Guests find the enthusiasm and dedication for a particular subject from this type of guide an inspiration, often returning from the game drive delighted to have been with someone who displays such a zest for a topic that they never realised could be so interesting and stimulating.

This type of guide will often return to camp having chalked up some good game sightings, too, as much time was spent looking for birds and driving so slowly that inevitably someone did spot lion, elephant, leopard, etc. They don't rush from waterhole to waterhole to see how much big game can be found. 'Normal' guides often miss a lot between waterholes as they tend to guide under self-inflicted pressure and neglect the rhythms of nature.

A number of years ago I was conducting a four day walking safari with a group, most of whom had come for big game experiences. There were also two ladies from the Tree Society, one of them none other than Meg Coates Palgrave, who lives, eats, drinks and sleeps **trees**! At first there was a bit of pressure and tension from the 'Big Game' people as we stopped every 25 metres for Meg to study the leaves, bark, flowers and pods of certain plants. This was accompanied by a never-ending flow of interesting facts about the uses of the particular specimen, Meg's eyes bright and filled with fire and enthusiasm while she bubbled away as if she would never see this plant again! She would then proceed to anchor a branch down with thin nylon ropes pegged into the ground, set up her tripod, camera and flash and methodically take vertical and horizontal shots of these living plant specimens. During this lengthy process everyone else stood around peering through their binoculars hoping that something as exciting as an impala would come by.

Meg couldn't even begin to understand why anyone would want to see things like elephant that disfigured her beloved trees. She is a very strong personality and it was difficult at first to keep her happy as well as the others. As the safari progressed, we began to have some very good wildlife sightings. The unsurpassed elephant bulls of Mana Pools gave us some incredible displays and experiences. This resulted in the game-orientated guests becoming content and relaxed and beginning to show an interest in what caused the enthusiasm of this eccentric woman.

When we drove to the airstrip on the last day, Meg tested everyone on the various trees of the park. In the course of the safari they had learnt and could recognize over twenty different species of tree. The whole group subsequently joined the Tree Society! They had expanded their horizons and now had a new subject to appreciate in nature.

Some years ago while staying at a lodge above the Victoria Falls on the Zambian side of the Zambezi, my wife and I decided to accompany the afternoon walk, which was to be on one of the larger islands. Our guide was to be Bob Stjernstedt.

An American honeymoon couple, who had been on safari for ten days and not so much as looked at a boring old bird, joined us. As we chugged up the river in an old banana boat, we studied Bob with interest as he lovingly paged through a well-used, dogeared bird book, peering intently at each page through a pair of bifocals which rested near the end of his nose. His sandalled feet were entombed in a pair of woollen socks, in which were holes of varying sizes, advertising hairy toes and thin anklebones.

When we reached the island, Bob set off in a world of his own, contentedly wandering beneath a tall canopy of riverine trees, whistling various birdcalls. These were soon answered by jealous males who swooped down to the nearest branch and excitedly called back to this imposter. They entertained us with their territorial displays. From his tattered khaki shorts Bob extracted an old pocket tape recorder and he accompanied his whistles with various taped birdcalls. We felt we were with the Pied Piper or St Francis as we explored an island within which Bob knew every nest and where he pointed out various young birds and well-camouflaged owls. He whistled along with the various songsters, interpreting their calls to rhyme with various English sayings.

'The eccentric guide'

It mattered not that we hadn't encountered a single mammal on the entire walk as Bob enthralled us with his antics and genuine love and understanding of birds to which he had such a great affinity.

We became firm friends with the honeymoon couple who subsequently asked us to arrange their next safari some two years later. Their one request was to go back to the same camp so that they could 'birdwatch' with Bob! I have spent many a night around campfires with people who have been out with Bob, comparing stories about his eccentric qualities, unknown to him as he pursues a study that has been the soul of his life. How many people have had their eyes opened by Bob to the joys of birdwatching and now have a new interest that can be pursued in the wilds, a garden or a big city?

It would be impossible not to mention another total eccentric - Jeff Stutchbury! This man was not besotted by a 'single' interest in the bush, but by them all! Jeff's passions were trees, birds, elephants, buffalo, fishing, water, solitude, his wife, sons, sunsets and, last but not least, photography. Everything that he did in life was done with maximum energy, great gusto and a lot of unusual noises that accompanied his antics. You could see Jeff had spent a long and hard life exposed to the African elements. He had been a crocodile hunter, crocodile farmer, big game hunter, warden in national parks, policeman, soldier, farmer, fisherman, safari guide and world-class photographer before cancer stole a life from which he took twenty-five hours of each day. A charming and mischievous smile and twinkling eyes highlighted a weatherbeaten face, always below a large-brimmed straw hat during the day.

Jeff looked the part of a 'white hunter' from bygone days. His tawny hair was swept back, and a well-groomed beard gave his face even more character. He was lean and strong with legs like mopane trunks and wrinkled knees like an old bull elephant. He also projected as much presence as one!

Jeff was extremely territorial, disliked and couldn't comprehend anything modern or urban. He was genuinely uncomfortable when out of the bush, but continued to give off a tremendous aura from his powerful personality wherever he was. There were absolutely no grey areas in his life. There was no room for compromise and because of this there were a few people who didn't appreciate him. Most people who met Jeff fell under his spell. He was completely devoted and dedicated to all forms of wildlife and their preservation.

Jeff and his wife Veronica were pioneers in wildlife guiding and photographic safaris in Zimbabwe. They built and managed a number of safari camps and lodges, which soon became sought out by visitors from many parts of the world because of this couple's sincere devotion to wildlife and tourism. As talented as Jeff was in creating the magic of Africa, so, too, was Veronica in ensuring that the management of their various camps was faultless.

To see Jeff behind a camera was an experience in itself. He would get so excited at taking what must have been his millionth lilac-breasted roller photo, that anyone would have thought he had just discovered the bird and was about to make it known to the world of science. His camera seemed to operate like a cowboy's revolver in the movies, the ones that never seem to run out of bullets. He received such a kick out of his quest for a good photograph that his mesmerised guests would watch him and not the animal or bird that he was capturing on his umpteenth camera. (Because of his active and adventurous life, most of his cameras had short life-spans!) His guests loved passing rolls of film across to him when it appeared that he was about to run out. If Jeff had finished his last roll of film and there was no spare film around while something exciting was happening in his viewfinder, he would emit sounds like a wounded buffalo.

One afternoon when I happened to be with Jeff on one of his custom-made game viewing boats in a quiet creek in Matusadona National Park on Lake Kariba, we spotted a leopard walking along the edge of the lake. Jeff became so excited that I thought we would have to get the first aid box out to treat him. I watched the four clients who were with us. They hardly glanced at the leopard as they were so spellbound by this man's *genuine* enthusiasm and appreciation of this secretive spotted cat.

Jeff also loved to create a crisis which made his guests feel they really were in darkest Africa. These incidents ranged from getting stuck in the mud, which resulted in everyone pushing the vehicle and being covered by copious layers of Africa's brown paint to hand cranking his old Land Rover, which always seemed not to start when there was a breeding herd of elephant around or on departing from a lion kill. Because Jeff was totally consumed with a passion for all that was wild, he gave his clients experiences they would never forget. He was a true showman without trying to be one. His eccentric behaviour was always totally genuine. He certainly was not a guide whose name a former client would forget!

There are not many guides who have made it into this category: you can't learn to be one, you can only be born one! Those who are not true eccentrics and try to emulate them, only make fools of themselves. Make the most of the personality and talents that you have been given. Be yourself and people will appreciate you for what you are and what you have to share with them.

'Remember your character is your destiny'

Chapter 3

Where to Begin

'That which is bitter to endure is often sweet to remember.'

The easiest way of joining the safari industry is to find a friend, relation, friend of a friend, or some contact who can put you in touch with a safari operator for an interview. This often helps a lot more than trying to get a job 'in cold blood'. If you have been set up for an interview through a friend or contact, don't forget their name is on the line for having recommended you; always try to uphold it.

There are various privately run guide training schools throughout Southern Africa (see Appendix A on p.224 for contact details) which offer comprehensive courses on all aspects of guiding, with courses varying from a few weeks to a few months. Successful candidates will come away with a diploma, which is useful when attempting to join the industry.

Beware, however, as there are some guide training and environmental education companies that have extremely low standards, morals and ethics.

If you have no contact at all, only an all-consuming desire to become a guide, visit the local Tour and Safari Operators Association. Ask them for a list of all their members and addresses. Write off to all or a select few - you are bound to get at least one reply. These associations also have a monthly newsletter with an advertisement section in which safari vehicles, rifles, camping equipment, etc. are offered for sale, and ads from various safari companies seeking camp management, caterers, guides, etc. appear. There is also a section, 'Situations Wanted', where you can advertise with your qualifications and personal details.

This is a much sought-after industry, so don't be disappointed if you meet with a few dead ends and frustrations. Don't give up. Keep badgering the companies for which you would really like to work: eventually they will have a place and they should be quite impressed by your perseverance and constant applications.

Alternatively, go into a local tour operator or travel agent and collect as many brochures as you can on the various camps, lodges and safari operations in the country. Go home and read them all. You should be able to glean from these glossy pages the type of company for which you would like to work.

The best approach is always in person. It is so easy for the safari operator to throw your posted application into 'file thirteen' or for the secretary to reply with a one liner, thanking you for your application, but informing you that they are fully staffed for that season.

Build up your courage and go out there and knock on doors. There is a very good chance that you will get to see the boss or make contact with the secretary. This is at least a foot in the door and one step closer to your new profession.

'Persist'

Your Future

Always try to be entirely honest with yourself and determine exactly why you want this kind of job. Can you picture yourself as a guide in twenty years' time when you have a spouse and a string of children? Do you want to make guiding a profession, or do you only want to do it for a few years?

Have you any formal education, degree, diploma or trade that you can fall back on once you find there is no glamour and glory to an eighteen-hour day, constantly around clients, without a personal and social life? Guiding often entails working on Christmas morning, taking

'Look ahead'

night drives on New Year's Eve while your buddies are all having a good party at the local bush pub! You are often at your busiest over public holidays and weekends. You will be away from family and friends for long periods. You can't just pop down the road to go and watch a movie, sit around listening to music or visit friends. You are committed to being in the bush, with a variety of different clients of diverse nationalities. You will be working in close contact with the same staff for months on end; friction is common.

I missed both my brothers' weddings and a few family funerals, and our first two children were induced to fit in with safaris! Guiding is far from an eight-to-five job. If you are not sure what you want out of guiding as a vocation, give it serious thought. You will only be wasting someone else's time and money, not to mention your own.

During your eighteen-hour day, while your clients are resting in the afternoon, there are always broken vehicles, waterpumps, boat engines, toilets, showers, boilers, generators and trailers to repair; cooler boxes to clean and fill, ice to break, safari vehicles to clean and get ready. Don't think that the other staff are there to do the menial chores, while you parade around in your starched, khaki uniform or lie in your room reading your favourite 'Western'! When you become a learner guide, you are lower than hyena turds in the eyes of the long-standing guides under whom you may be apprenticed . They had to do all that they expect of you when they were training and wouldn't bat an eyelid at doing it again now, should the situation arise.

'Sweat is the cologne of accomplishment'

It is wise and highly recommended to get a relevant degree or diploma. A trade in the numerous forms of mechanical engineering is invaluable in the safari industry. Most of the vehicles and equipment with which you will be working will often have 'a lot of character'! You could find yourself spending more time beneath the vehicle or under its bonnet than in its seat! There is very seldom a day in a safari camp when something hasn't broken down or doesn't require attention. There are also roads to repair, firebreaks and boreholes to maintain, supplies to collect. This doesn't mean driving down to the local grocery store. It is often a one-day round trip on bad roads and woe betide if you don't bring back all the supplies that the 'matriarchal caterer' had on her shopping list!

This is going to be one of the biggest decisions in your life, so think about it very seriously. Seek out the advice of those you consider to be wise and sensible. Look around at the various safari operators whom you may know and ask yourself if you want to be like them in twenty years' time.

Qualifications

You don't necessarily have had to grow up in the bush, on a farm or be related to Courtney Selous to qualify for entry into this profession. A number of good guides have come straight out of city life after finishing school or university.

First and foremost you need a *genuine* appreciation of the great outdoors and all its treasures. It helps to be *observant* and have an *enquiring* mind.

'Be instructed by everything you see and hear'

Secondly, you need a *positive attitude*. This is one of the most important factors in any line of work, be it guiding or hairdressing. It is of importance to all around you, your peers, employer, company, staff and most of all to the people who pay your salary, not your boss, but the *clients* who pay your salary. You are there for them, not they for you.

'A misty morning does not mean a cloudy day'

There is nothing more refreshing than being in the company of someone positive, and nothing more draining and debilitating than being with someone negative. I am sure you have been unfortunate enough to encounter this unpleasant breed. Their faces, over the years, have even taken on the sour, down turned lip look, from a lifetime of whinging and whining. Stay clear of them, as they will drain your energy and make everything around you appear gloomy! You will not get far in life if you associate with this group of humans!

'Don't walk away from negative people, run away from them!'

- A good command of **English** is essential. Being able to speak other languages is a great advantage. Most countries require learner guides to have a minimum education of grade 12 or standard 10 or form 5. Should you have a Bachelor of Science degree or a recognized wildlife diploma, it will stand you in good stead.
- A clean **driver's licence** is an obvious requirement. Initially, a lot of time will be spent behind the wheel on camp chores and taking game drives.
- You can never do enough **first aid** and **medic's courses** throughout your career as a guide. With this valuable knowledge and experience, you may be able to save life or limb someday, be it from an animal injury or an overturned safari vehicle. A first aid certificate is an important asset to add to your list of credentials.
- Most countries in Africa require you to be a **citizen** or **resident** to register as a trainee guide. Some companies do, however undertake to arrange work permits for nonresidents.

What Type of Safari Company to Choose

You may be desperate to get into the industry, but be patient and wise in choosing your employer, tutor and mentor. There is a fine balance in guiding, so ensure that your foundation is the best you could wish for, even if you have to wait a few more months before you can get a position with a ***reputable*** company and guide.

Each company has its own fingerprinting. Just by looking at their dress and the way their staff display themselves, you can often correctly guess which safari company various guides work for. This obviously stems from the top and the way the owner and management want to portray their company to the public and all around them. If the owner goes around all day without a shirt, barefoot and with hair tied back in a ponytail, his young guides and apprentices will often endeavour to emulate him.

When you first start out as an apprentice guide you will be like a piece of blotting paper, absorbing all that is being said and done around you. This is where a lot of good and bad habits will be picked up. Your superiors will be your role models. You will learn to portray wildlife one way or another: either enthusiastically and honestly, or as 'the last of the big game hunters'. Once you have been fingerprinted, it is difficult to change the way you project yourself. Should you seek employment later in life with another company, you will often be viewed against the type of people who trained you. Remember, 'birds of a feather flock together' – it's your life, your choice and your future!

'Yob clone'

The Job Interview

Treat this interview as you would any other. Just because you are applying for a job in the bush doesn't mean that you have to go dressed as if you have been in the jungle for six months without a change of clothes. First impressions count. But equally, you don't have to go dressed up in a suit. A clean set of clothes that don't make an outrageous statement is all you need. Always arrive for your interview early.

During your interview, don't just sit there answering questions about yourself. Ask as many questions as you can think of about the job, the area, kinds of mammal, bird, vehicles, origin of clients, what is to be expected of you, what you need to bring, etc. Show some interest and enthusiasm. If you are shy, dull and boring, that is how the interviewer will imagine you to be with the clients. It isn't difficult to teach someone about wildlife if they have a desire to learn, but it is well nigh impossible to change someone's personality, especially from being an introvert to being vibrant and sincere with guests. If you don't know the difference between a pied crow and a pied kingfisher, but are relaxed and comfortable around people, can create conversation and are keen and willing to learn, you stand a better chance of getting the job than someone who has great knowledge but can't put it across and isn't people orientated.

Never exaggerate your knowledge or achievements at your interview. Don't make out that you are competent at something if you aren't. It will soon become apparent and the last thing that your employer wants is a chancer. They are two a penny.

'You won't impress by your dress'

What is Expected of You?

Congratulations, you have been given the job; it will be a whole new way of life for you. It is normal to be nervous and apprehensive. Often nervous energy is good for you and makes you perform better. You arrive at your new place of employ, you aren't sure what you should be doing and where you should be. It feels like everyone is watching you to see if you are up to scratch. Everyone else seems so knowledgeable, confident, self-assured and in place. It is like starting at a new school. Don't worry, it's all quite normal. Just relax and take a lesson from nature: 'go with the flow'.

As mentioned earlier, you are the lowest in the pile, you are the 'gopher' (*go for* this and *go for* that) yes, a general dogsbody. You are an apprentice learner guide, go and ask any apprentice mechanic, builder, fitter and turner, carpenter etc. about the type of jobs that they were given when they first started. It takes a while to climb that pile!

> *'The only place where success comes before work,*
> *is in the dictionary'*

Don't expect to be driving all the good-looking tourists around in your first week. You may be asked to dig long-drop toilets, service the tractor, clean the toilets, assist in washing up the dishes in the kitchen. Your employers will be looking at your attitude to doing these menial chores. Attack them with great gusto!

> *'That which is bitter to endure is often sweet to remember'.*

While digging the 'long drop', collect the various blindworms, centipedes, termite fungi and insect larvae that you encounter and ask the other guides to identify them for you. You *always* have the opportunity to learn, even when down in the bottom of a newly dug 'long drop'! As you wash the dishes, find the mud wasps' nests in the kitchen, get to know the kitchen staff and let them see that washing pots and plates is not beneath you, ask as many questions as you can, from whomsoever you can, to get an idea of how things work in camp and out in the field.

Always be up and about, washed and dressed *before* the professional guide under whom you are apprenticed, even if this means 04:30 in the morning. Things begin to happen very early in safari camps, often long before dawn. There is nothing worse than a guide who stumbles across to the morning campfire, bleary-eyed, with uncombed hair, looking wild and dishevelled. The clients have been enjoying the warm flames for the past twenty minutes, eagerly discussing the various night sounds that they have heard, only to be joined by this apparition who finds it difficult to rise on time. From the time you join this industry to the time you leave, everyone around you will be expecting you to be dedicated to nature and a healthy outdoor life. If this is your choice of work, live up to their expectations.

'The long drop to reality'

Chapter 4

The Learning Curve

'Who dares to teach must never cease to learn.'

There is no limit to the amount that you can learn in such a diverse field as natural history. You will hardly scrape the surface in a lifetime of what our rich environment in Africa has to teach us. There is so much to learn, all the mammals, big and small; don't forget that mice, rats and bats are also mammals. There can be over 120 species of mammal alone in some game reserves. You need to learn their habits, habitat, breeding, feeding, vocalisations, etc. Then there is the world of birds, their calls, breeding plumages, nests, eggs, migratory behaviour, feeding, territorial behaviour, etc. The massive family of insects, both above and underground is waiting to be studied. There are grasses, shrubs, creepers, trees, their pods, seeds, flowers, and pollination. Reptiles...amphibians...geology...astronomy - and so the long list continues. Once you are familiar with all the above in your particular area, don't forget there are many other climatic and habitat differences throughout the country with their endemic species, not to mention the rest of Africa! It is mind boggling and enough to make even the most learned feel incredibly humble!

'To acquire knowledge one must study,
to acquire wisdom one must observe.'

So you thought you had left a lifetime of learning behind at school? Don't worry this is far more stimulating and exciting than pi r squared, algebra and science symbols. Isn't it a great thought that you have chosen a vocation which offers an inexhaustible supply of things to discover and share with your fellow man?

Learn all you can while your brain is open and uncluttered, devoid of the baggage it will accumulate as life progresses! (By these I mean new responsibilities to a spouse, children, their health and education.) One day you will be promoted to head guide or camp manager, and you will be accountable to the owners and the clients for much more than just finding a lot of animals. The camp supplies, vehicle maintenance, staff problems, client arrival and departure logistics, national park relationships, finance, profits, plus many other responsibilities will be carried on your shoulders. Apparently this is called progress. You may acquire your own safari company. You now have all of the above responsibilities, plus meetings with the bank manager, to whom you are beholden, time to be spent with bookkeepers and accountants, plus organisation of marketing and brochures. Don't forget you also have a family life to attend to. So make the *most* of the years in which you can wander around the bush with very few worries! Learn and absorb as much as you can, both physically and mentally, while you have the opportunity.

'And they call this progress'

'Brain power without will power is no power.'

When I started guiding, Zimbabwe had just obtained its independence after fifteen years of guerilla war. Tourists were as rare as royal game. We had very few clients to look after. I was extremely fortunate in that my boss and professional guide encouraged me to go off alone for hours on end to learn from observation.

I tried to learn two new plants each day. I collected these plants and did some bird watching as I explored the elephant highways that connected all the major waterholes through massive teak and acacia forests. I shall never forget that wonderful smell from the tons of dried elephant dung that line these ancient paths like a carpet of underfelt. I vividly remember the comfort and spring in my step caused by this thick, golden carpet of poorly digested bark, twigs, leaves and seeds, the excitement and anticipation of meeting up with a herd of elephant coming the opposite way and feeling the immense presence that they command from their size and wisdom. I often watched what seemed like a never-ending parade of these magnificent beasts from the safety of the highest strong limb of a well-positioned teak tree.

If I saw a sable antelope pass dung, I would walk over to the spot once the animal had moved away, pick up its fresh dung, study its colour, shape and make up, place a few pellets in a plastic bag and take it back to add to my dung collection. How different they looked in real life from their sketched depictions in the mammal book! And so my life continued for three years. Our only responsibilities were to ensure that our few clients left satisfied from a good wildlife experience.

After three years the boss I had idolised left the country. I now had to step into his huge boots. I was faced with the lodge manager who wanted to know why we were over budget on repairs and maintenance. What did he expect from a fleet of Land Rovers that would have easily made it into any British museum? Anyway, who thought up this thumb-suck budget in the first place?

Once a month the group operations manager would come around to inspect all the properties that the company owned. He was clawing and kicking his way up the 'corporate ladder' and wanted 'big bottom-line results'. I always knew when he was about to arrive, as our lodge manager would break out in boils on his face from nerves. Be mindful of the direction you take as a guide. Don't get too bogged down with all the paperwork that it can create if you let it. Keep it simple - your brain needs to be uncluttered in order to guide properly.

Years later, when we owned a safari camp in Mana Pools National Park, I remember going out on game walks with my ears flapping. No, not for the sound of an elephant squeal, rhino snort or lion growl, but for the throb from 'old blues' honest diesel engine. It was meant to be back from its resupply five hours ago. What if it didn't get back to camp that evening? We would have no ice, no eggs for breakfast tomorrow, and there would be no vegetables in camp. Had it broken down, or possibly rolled? We couldn't afford to have another vehicle out of action as we already had 'the brick' waiting for its reconditioned gear box. What was plan B if 'old blue' didn't return? All this would be going through my mind as I walked and talked about wildlife, just like a 'wind-up guide'!

It is not possible to guide well if you don't have someone else to take care of all the little and big admin hassles. Guiding safely and productively needs a clear and uncluttered mind. You need to be thinking like a wild animal, not like an accountant.

Where and How to Learn?

The greatest place to learn about wildlife and its intricate ways is to enrol as a student in the 'Bush University'. There are many in each country. They offer the biggest classroom imaginable; lectures are in session twenty-four hours of each day. The fees are low and the only entrance requirement is a will to learn and observe. There are no examinations to be written, no degrees with which to walk away. There is only the personal satisfaction of being a student of this great university and learning to understand the patterns of life.

'The bush university'

Books

'Out of the books,
into the wilds'

There are many ways to learn some of the secrets that wildlife keeps hidden from modern man. I have heard many guides say after breakfast or lunch, "I am off to my room to read and learn". Sure, you will learn quite a lot from the incredible array of natural history books that is now available. But don't forget the words of North America's greatest naturalist John Muir when he said, *"books are merely stepping stones to where other minds have been"*.

In your study of wildlife, be objective and enquiring, read as much as you can, but don't take everything that you read to be gospel! Someone may have studied sable antelope in the Taita Hills of eastern Kenya and obtained a doctorate from this study and then written a book. All the facts and observations on the behaviour of those sable do not necessarily comply with the sable that live in your neck of the woods. This applies especially to elephant behaviour, which can differ dramatically within a single country.

Unless you have a photographic memory you cannot hope to remember all that a book has to teach by reading it from cover to cover. If you have the time to read, go ahead, as it will give you a good idea of how any particular animal functions, but it does not compare with personal observation in the field!

You can't learn all your trees by reading a massive plant book from beginning to end; the same applies to birds, stars, insects, reptiles, grasses, etc. The best thing to do with books is to use them as a reference after you have watched a certain animal, bird, insect, etc. and its behaviour has intrigued you, or someone has asked a question to which you did not know the answer. Look it up in the relevant books and then write personal notes on your observations and the pertinent points that you gleaned from the reference books. You will see that most books have conflicting opinions and data on a particular subject anyway. Writing down your newfound knowledge may seem tedious, but it is a good way of ensuring that it sinks in, hopefully for life.

*'The art of observation is through participation.
Don't be an armchair naturalist'.*

Video and Wildlife Documentaries

How privileged we are to have such incredible wildlife exposure from the numerous videos and documentaries that are available these days. In one hour we are treated to the highlights of three years of filming and intense study by a small group of dedicated film-makers and naturalists who bring amazing wildlife sequences into the homes of millions of people around the world. Should you have access to such videos and can watch them on a video machine, they are a great tool for learning about various wildlife topics.

Learning from Others

A great deal of knowledge can be obtained by following as many bush boffins around as possible. Here you have the opportunity to learn, in a short period, information that has taken them a lifetime of observation and interpretation.

'Tapping years of experience'

Once again, don't take as fact everything you hear. Sieve out the information and theories and make your own assessments. Wildlife topics are like religion and politics; each person has his or her own theory and belief. Some of the old hunters and characters who have been living in the wilds for most their lives find it difficult to agree with the findings of modern-day wildlife researchers. They still abide by the stories of elephant graveyards, drunken elephants and stomach rumbling. You will hear from some of them about honey guides leading baboons to beehives. White dung always indicates hyena because they eat so many bones. Kudu with wide horns live in the vleis and eat grass, while kudu with a narrow rack of horns live in the thick bush and eat leaves.

So the list of myths and beliefs which some of the 'old school' naturalists will take to the grave with them goes on. These stories have been passed on by some of the very early hunters and explorers and because of the awe in which these men were held, no one has ever thought of refuting some of their theories.

Targets and Notes

Set yourself a target to learn something new each day, be it a mammal, bird or plant. Look it up and make notes on your findings. This will increase your knowledge and keep your brain active and stimulated. Many guides learn just enough to get by on, their learning curve flattens out and then begins to drop slightly, while their social skills develop and get them by.

Make notes on unusual sightings and observations, with dates and location. These notes will be of valuable assistance when discussing an unusual event with an interested party. Years later when looking back through your notes you will be amazed at how many observations you made that you had forgotten about. Try and record each year: when the first rain fell, the appearance of the crinum lilies, the birth of the first impala, the arrival of the first Carmine Bee-eaters and when they began to drill their nesting sites, how long it took before the nest was complete and when the first dowdy plumaged youngster showed itself from its darkened home. Record when each species of acacia flushed with flower, which month their pods grew, when they dropped and what creatures ate them. How long after a downpour of rain did the winged termites appear? How many species of bird, reptile and animal fed off them? Record rainfall, temperature, waterhole, lake and river levels.

So many things are interconnected in nature and if there is an unusual event, you may be able to correlate it to a drought, flood, cold winter, fire, etc. It is interesting to look back through your notes over the years and see how the dates of each event differ. These targets and notes assist in making your work more stimulating, and show that you are not just doing the job because you have a driver's licence and can speak English!

Specialist Topic

As time goes by you may find that you have a talent or affinity to a particular subject or species. This may be birds, plants, spiders, photography or a particular mammal. There are so many different areas in which people discover a lifelong interest. Pursue your interests and strong points. Endeavour to be one of the best on the topic, but never forget that not everyone gets as turned on by your chosen subject as you do. While you could sit all day watching your study group of baboons, you will find that the average tourist will want to move on after fifteen minutes and find something else to look at and photograph. Don't treat them as the unenlightened; they are just normal people out for a good time on their safari holiday.

If you are fortunate enough to take out someone who shares your interest, you can have a field day, but make sure it isn't with everyone else on the main safari activity of the day. They haven't come on your game drive to listen to the two of you waxing lyrical about baboons and their behaviour for three hours.

'Bobboring!'

When there is a quiet time in camp and guests are having a rest after breakfast or lunch, take this opportunity to sneak off with your enthusiast on a special outing. It will do you both the world of good. You will be stimulated to have found someone who shares your main interest and he or she will feel privileged and spoilt that you went out of your way to share and discuss your findings and observations.

Try not to become too obsessed with a single topic and blind to all else around you. Single-minded guides with tunnel vision can become a bore if they converse intensely on only one subject. Everything has its place in the great web of life, so attempt to put across as big a picture as possible.

Slide Shows

As a guide you have the perfect opportunity to encounter and record some amazing animal behaviour and settings. If you are keen on photography, as most guides become, share these experiences with your guests in evening slide shows. It enables them to relax and enjoy a topic in which they obviously have an interest. That is why they are in your safari camp. In this informal setting they may ask a variety of questions - which will broaden their knowledge and yours.

This little extra time spent a few evenings a week will make you more confident in public speaking, and more relaxed with people. It is always daunting to address an audience. The good thing about slide shows is that you give your presentation when it's dark and you normally stand behind your audience.

There is so much one can say about a wildlife slide. Try to make your presentation educational. Having stunning pictures that take everyone's breath away is a bonus, but you don't want to state the obvious, "a nice buffalo in the evening light on the banks of the river". Explain what type of buffalo it is, how it differs from the other species of buffalo and where they occur. Point out the oxpecker perched on its back and describe their symbiotic role. Talk about the cattle egrets at the buffalo's feet. Dispel the myth of its name of tickbird, and explain why it is around the animal's feet. Let your audience leave having learnt something and not only in admiration of your photographic talents.

Off Season

A number of safari camps close during the rains and in off-season. If you are employed in one of these camps, use this valuable time for improving your guiding techniques and knowledge. Get out there, find a course to go on, spend time in different parts and parks of your country, eventually moving further afield to other countries so you can see what they offer the visitor as far as wildlife opportunities and standards are concerned. You will then realize what you are competing against, how much more effort you may need to put into giving guests a better wildlife

'Head off season'

experience. Try to seek temporary employment at another safari camp during the low season. It is always good to get fresh ideas and share your own with like-minded people. By visiting other camps, parks and countries, you broaden your horizon and can speak with first-hand experience on these areas and operations. These travels may also make you appreciate your own camp and area more, especially if you were getting burnt out and stale, having lost some of the original enthusiasm you had when you first came to work there.

Black Belt

Acquiring wildlife knowledge is very similar to climbing the ladder of the martial arts, where the main aim of students is to achieve black-belt status. Young guides can't wait to get their professional guide's licence. Armed with this piece of paper they feel they have acquired local and international recognition. True, a lot of hard work, time and study goes into obtaining this licence, but you haven't reached the top of the guiding pyramid when you become eligible for it. You certainly go out there bursting with pride and energy, dying to test your strength and knowledge.

In the martial arts there are ten levels of black belt to achieve after qualifying for the first black belt. Very few ever get to 'tenth Dan'. As time progresses and the students proceed up the martial ladder acquiring more black belts (Dans), this does not mean they are getting any stronger or younger. It means they are becoming more in tune with the cycle of life, a higher level of perception, timing, self-belief, and a clear understanding of how everything works. Guiding is very much like this; the more time you spend in the wilds with people, the more confident you become in your environment, with your fellow man and yourself. You know how to portray the wildlife story and create the magic. This doesn't mean rattling off all the Latin names of every tree, bird and mammal on the safari and impressing everyone with your 'immense knowledge'. The young black belts possibly have more facts and figures to throw out but haven't quite fine-tuned all the different wavelengths that go into making the big picture.

Never lose sight of the fact that you never stop learning and will be merely scratching the surface of wildlife and its diversity in an entire lifetime. You have become an ambassador to wildlife and the environment; portray your valuable subject honestly and enthusiastically!

'Who dares to teach must never cease to learn.'

'You never reach your peak'

Chapter 5

Preparation

'Failing to prepare, is preparing to fail'

You have settled into your niche in the pecking order of your new safari camp. You have humbly accepted that you are at the bottom of the pile. What have you been employed to do? You didn't think it was to dig 'long drops', wash up pots in the kitchen, check if there are spare loo rolls in all the toilets, take the rubbish bins down to the pit and fix all the flat tyres in the workshop. But you have completed all these chores with a positive attitude; you have followed the 'learned' guides around like a shadow. You are familiar with the road network and your boss is ready to unleash you on your first group of clients! Your first solo game drive.

Here are a few hints on what equipment you need, and how to prepare before you depart on this much-awaited event. Keep this little saying in the back of your mind: *'Failing to Prepare, is Preparing to Fail'*. That's the last thing any of us want to do! Loss of face is one of the biggest fears we all have. By failing to prepare correctly, you can lose a lot of face, but worse than that, you can deprive your clients of the time and precious opportunity to interact and enjoy the wildlife they came so far to see.

*Remember the old military adage of the **Seven P's**:*
'Proper planning and preparation, prevents, piss poor performance.'

What do you need? Let's start with:

Clothes

You don't need to be dressed like a model for *'Hunting Magazine'*, neither do you want to look like you have been in the workshop all morning. A clean shirt and shorts, preferably green or khaki, a good hat and a clean pair of bush shoes are all you really need. Try to make as little statement as possible from your appearance and dress; rather let your guiding talents make the statement. Mature clients are not impressed with a guide who saunters up in a pair of blown-out track shoes, frayed and tattered boxer shorts, a white-water rafting T-shirt, a peak cap worn back to front and a cigarette dangling from a down-turned mouth.

Wear sunglasses by all means, as your eyes need protection from the constant exposure to the harsh African sun and dust. When meeting people, take them off, your eyes will tell them more about you than any other part of your body, let them see who is really taking them on this much-awaited safari. When introducing yourself to each client, look him or her in the eye and spend a few seconds with them as you repeat and memorise their names. A smile and a friendly, open face go a long way. A genuine welcome will make them feel relaxed as they eagerly await your instruction of where to sit in the vehicle or boat.

Personal Hygiene

Make sure you wash regularly. Greasy hair and an unshaven face don't impress anyone, but they will tell people a few things about yourself even before you open your mouth. If you have a problem with BO, use a deodorant. Be conscious of bad breath. Clean your teeth after each meal. You don't want to be explaining the wonders of your area with the spinach from lunch wedged between your teeth for all to see.

'Oh no, B.O.'

Binoculars

There is very little more important for a guide or a tourist on a wildlife safari than a *good* pair of binoculars. This is probably the most important tool in guiding. It will literally enhance wildlife sightings tenfold. A guide needs a clear and workable set of binoculars to identify animals that are unrecognisable at a distance. It is almost impossible to identify and appreciate birds without binoculars.

Carry your set with you *everywhere*, from the time you wake up till you go to bed. They will come in handy at meals when tame camp birds visit feeding trays and birdbaths. Animals may be down at the camp waterhole; you should be able to identify them. It is a lame excuse to say, ' Sorry I can't see what animal is drinking, my binos are in my room or the safari vehicle'. At night you may have hyena or a honey badger come around the camp kitchen or dining area. A look through your binoculars will give your guests a far better perspective of these interesting nocturnal characters. In the evening a glance at the moon through binoculars will show the craters and ancient larval seas, so share this sight with your guests. Use binoculars to illustrate some of the moons of Jupiter, or colourful and interesting constellations.

You won't find a carpenter without a saw, a mechanic without spanners, or an accountant without a calculator. These are all tools of their trades. Imagine taking a game drive and having to ask your clients for a look through their binoculars in order to identify a creature. There are a number of guides who do that. Basically, it shows a lack of pride and interest.

Keep your binoculars clean and in good working order. Sometimes clients don't have binoculars (sadly), and you may offer them yours to enjoy a particular sighting. You wouldn't want them looking through optics covered with dust and greasy fingerprints.

I have owned many binoculars over the years. As a young guide I couldn't afford any of the renowned names, so purchased what I could afford. They were invariably on special offer at the local camera store. I would leave the store so proud of my new acquisition and 'good deal'. Following an accidental drop to the ground, an unplanned bang against the roll bars and a few spots of rain, my great bargain was as much use as an ashtray on the back of a motorbike. The prisms in cheap binoculars are easily knocked out of line, resulting in blurred vision. The cost to repair them is often more than their original cost.

There is nothing to beat a *good* set of binoculars. Unfortunately, it is the chicken-and-egg situation; when you start out guiding you can't even afford to buy the case of a good set.

There are basically three makes of binoculars that will last you a lifetime. The best makes are *Leica, Zeiss* and *Swarovski*. They cost between US$600 and

$1 000. Extremely expensive, but they will become your closest bush companion for many years. Most of these makes are shockproof and water protected. If you can scrape up enough money to make such a purchase, it will be one of the best investments you will make in your guiding career.

There are other good makes which are not quite as expensive; these are **Nikon, Minolta, Canon** and **Pentax**. They have very good optics, but do not always take kindly to being dropped, especially if it is into water.

What size and power do you need? Size is a personal thing; you don't want a pair so big and heavy that they are cumbersome to carry with you everywhere you go. Alternatively, you don't want a little set that would only look good at the opera, as they have a very narrow field of vision. Avoid 'gimmick' binoculars such as those with auto focus or a zoom from 6 to 15 power; they are never as good as fixed glass and crystal.

Generally speaking, 8 x 30s tend to be the best all-round size. The first figure represents the binocular's magnification; they are magnified 8 times to that of your eyes' normal vision. The second figure represents the width of the glass or lenses of the front optics; in this case they are 30 millimetres in diameter. The wider this piece of glass, such as a 7 x 50, the more light will be let in to a 50mm front optic, this will enhance low light viewing. This is an advantage, but with it comes an unwieldy size.

Don't buy a pair of binoculars that are over 10 power. They are nearly impossible to hold still. The slightest hand tremor or wind will cause shake and hence unsteady vision. The unsuspecting are often sold such binoculars by a salesman on the pretext that they are the most powerful in the shop. A brief look out of the shop door at a car's number plate and sure enough, every scratch in the paint can be seen. Some time later, when proudly sitting in your safari vehicle with your new 15 x 60s slung around your aching neck, you await the opportunity to tell everyone what type of dung beetle landed on a warthog's dropping

'Zeiss is everything'

65

500 metres away. After straining to raise the binoculars to your eager eyes, you will be lucky if you see the warthog, let alone a dung beetle because of the shaky vision from your unmounted bioscope. Although there are a number of high-powered binoculars with image stabilizers to prevent shake and blurred vision, they are still gimmicky and will not beat a good pair of 8 x 30's or 10 x 40's.

A useful tip (learned through an expensive lesson): never clean the lenses of your binoculars with your shirt. The course material and fine dust will scratch the delicately coated lenses; and these scratches will soon impede the clarity of your expensive acquisition. Always use a soft, fine weave, micro-fibre cloth to clean your optics. They are specially made for camera and binocular lenses.

Knife

A Swiss army knife or Leatherman tool is invaluable to a guide. These small and practical knives come in very handy on any safari, if only to open drinks and wine at sunset. They come in all shapes and sizes. Their most useful attributes are a lock blade, saw, scissors, pliers, screwdriver, tweezers, corkscrew, can and bottle opener. It is amazing how many emergency repairs you can do on a safari vehicle with one of these well-made knives. Be watchful of imitations. They are invariably cheap, become blunt and break easily. You get what you pay for. There is little need for a long sheath knife. They often can't cut butter, and are impractical. They are favoured by macho guides to enhance a perceived image.

I have included a story where a guide's knife possibly saved a life. The story was sent to me by a guide from the Okavango Delta. It is written in his words, making it first hand and very real.

I was working at a camp in the north of the Okavango Delta at the time of the incident. I carried a short but strong Kershaw knife and it came in very handy when we did activities like fishing, lodge maintenance, cleaning and preparing fish for meals and camping wild on islands within the delta.

I was at the local bush airstrip when a plane landed to drop off some guests. Once the guests had disembarked, the plane took off with only the pilot on board. Shortly after take-off the plane crashed into some nearby trees. The aircraft landed on its roof and the pilot was trapped inside.

I ran to the crash site and first used the knife to help get rid of some of the glass from the windscreen, so I could get to the pilot, who was unconscious at the time. His safety harness was still on and we could not unbuckle it. The instrument panel was pushed forward completely and the pilot's legs were pinned between the seat and the panel.

> *I took the knife and started cutting away some of the hard plastic of the instrument panel to get his legs loose. I then cut the safety harness off so that we could get the pilot out of the plane.*
>
> *The pilot was badly injured and spent four months in hospital, but survived. If we did not have a knife with us to cut him loose, we would really have battled to get him out.*
>
> *We feel it is important for lodge managers working in the conditions that they do in the delta to carry a Leatherman with them. We have made it compulsory for our lodge managers to have one with them at all times.*

Reference Books

There are a number of useful books to take with you whenever you go out on safari. Firstly a good field guide to **birds**. Invariably you will see a bird that has everyone confused, or someone may question your identification of a certain species. You need your book and binoculars there and then to solve the mystery. Books are also useful as a visual tool when you describe the varied features and adaptations that birds have to their bills, wings and legs that slot them into so many niches, preventing inter-species competition.

A **mammal** field guide helps to show clients what certain elusive animals look like; they may have caught only a glimpse of the slender mongoose that ran across the road. If you have the space, it doesn't harm to have books on the local trees, reptiles, insects and wild flowers. There will always be someone who is happy to page through them while you are driving along or sitting at a waterhole.

Radio

These days, all safari operations should have radios. They are the lifeline to a safari camp for bookings, air charters and resupply orders. Of the utmost importance is instant access to the medical air rescue, should the need arise. Radios save a safari operation a lot of time and money. A HF (high frequency) radio is used for long-distance communications, possibly to your town office and medical air rescue operator. A VHF (very high frequency) radio is a variable short-range radio. Depending on the terrain and repeater stations, they can cover an average radius of about 80 kilometres. They are either fixed into a vehicle or are hand held, the latter being more versatile.

Radios are of immense benefit for communication between guides, camp managers, resupply drivers and all the other people who make up a safari operation. Should a vehicle break down, get stuck or have an accident, the radio offers instant access to help and assistance.

Before you leave on your safari, ensure that you have a VHF radio that *works,* as well as a *fully charged,* spare battery.

Medic's Pack

It can't be stressed enough how vitally important it is to have a well stocked and up-to-date medic's pack in your vehicle, boat, mokoro, canoe or walking pack. You must know its contents and how to use them. It is advisable to have the pack in a waterproof container to protect its contents from rain, waves (if in a boat), or when your canoe tips over. What is the use of a medic's box back in camp, when most accidents happen out in the field? This can be a vehicle accident or a wild animal injury. Say your vehicle gets into a skid on a gravel road, hits a tree, and three people are injured. Do you say to them, "Wait here while I run back to camp to get the medic's box"? You may think this point is exaggerated, but a high percentage of safari operators and camps do not take medic's packs on their drives or walks.

It is also pointless leaving the medic's bag in your vehicle if you take a group walking in the bush. Each trip into the wild is an unknown event, and even the best guide can't predict if something unusual is going to occur. Imagine what could happen if a buffalo got up from thick cover, unseen by the guide and the first three members of the walking party. He charges and knocks down the fourth person, who sustains severe injuries. What would the guide do with the client lying there traumatised and bleeding? Begin to tear everyone's clothes to pieces to make bandages and then run to the vehicle for the medic's box?

If the guide had a medic's bag in a backpack, he or she could get into action immediately, stem the bleeding with dressings and bandages, set up a drip, administer painkillers and radio camp for help. By

DON'T **EVER** LEAVE WITHOUT ME!

having instant access to this vital equipment you may be able to save life or limb one day. Carrying your medic's pack with you on all safaris is a small price to pay for this insurance. Accidents happen when least expected.

If you are a canoe guide or pole a mokoro, always ensure that your waterproof medic's box is tied inside your canoe. If your canoe were to be tipped over by a hippo and the passenger in the bow was injured, what use would your medic's box be if it wasn't tied in and waterproof?

These are **little** *things that can make a* **very big** *difference.*

In the mid-eighties, one of the Hwange safari operators was transferring an Australian couple to the airport from the safari camp which was situated deep within the national park. They were about half way to the airport when the guide, while driving fast, hit a hump in the road. The bolts that attached the seat frame to the vehicle were missing. On hitting the bump the clients and the seat lifted up, the husband holding on to the angle iron of the seat frame. When they landed back on the vehicle again, his little finger was crushed by the angle iron against the bodywork.

Imagine the pain. There was no medic's box in the vehicle! To make matters worse they ran out of petrol a few kilometres from the park headquarters. The guide had to run to the headquarters and borrow a vehicle to take the extremely distressed and traumatised client to Hwange hospital where his finger was amputated. The couple cancelled the rest of the safari and flew back to Australia. All this could have been avoided had a little attention been paid to a few small details. The vehicle, its seats and fuel level should have been checked, before departure, not by the mechanic, but by the guide. Ultimately the guide is the one who will be held responsible if something goes wrong. The medic's bag must be with you whenever you leave camp. None of these checks take much time, yet they can save a lot of trouble and trauma.

So, now you have your binos around your neck, medic's bag in the vehicle, radio clipped to your belt alongside your Swiss army knife, reference books in the front shelf of your vehicle and you are looking relatively presentable. You are nearly ready for your game drive.

Your Vehicle

- Ensure that it is *clean*, no cigarette ends, rubbish or bottles rolling around the floor and in the pockets behind the seats. If there are windows, make sure they have no fingerprints or blemishes. If you have been given the old 'banger' with torn upholstery on the seats, collect a few clean towels or blankets and cover them.
- *Blankets* are necessary on winter mornings and evenings, so that your freezing clients may cover themselves when that warm African sun is not around. Some of the more organised safari companies provide waterproof ponchos lined with a warm inner blanket.
- If the weather is hot, a *canvas roof canopy* helps shade the passengers from the harsh and uncomfortable African sun.
- During the rainy season, make sure your vehicle has as few leaks as possible. If *raincoats* or *ponchos* are available, take them along, or suggest that the guests bring their own.
- Check your *fuel* and ensure that it is more than adequate for what you intend to do.
- Check your *oil* and *water*.
- Make sure there is a spare *fan belt* behind the seat, which is the correct size for that particular vehicle.
- Ensure that you have sufficient *spanners* in the vehicle to carry out minor repairs should your vehicle break down.
- Always carry five litres of *water* in a container; it can come in handy in a variety of situations.
- Take along a *shovel* and *axe* in case you get stuck in sand or mud. These can be attached to the bull bars, along the side, or stowed in the rear of the vehicle.
- A strong *towrope* is always useful, even if only to pull someone else out of a sticky situation.
- If you are permitted to conduct night drives with a *spotlight*, ensure that it is in working order and that its red filter is in place.
- Check that you have a *spare tyre* and make sure it is not flat (which is a very common occurrence in a safari camp). The vehicle may have had a puncture on an earlier game drive with another guide, who changed to the spare. On returning to camp that evening, off went the guide to have a drink with the clients and nobody remembered to fix the flat tyre, now in the spare position. Spare tyres may also go flat in time if the last puncture was not properly repaired . So give it a good kick or hard hit with the wheel spanner to ensure it has sufficient air.

- Check that the vehicle has a *jack* and that it works. There may be a hydraulic jack, which is low on oil and cannot lift a heavy safari vehicle. Make sure you have a good sized chock of wood on which to place the base of your jack to prevent it sinking into the mud as you jack up your vehicle, bogged down to its axles. Familiarise yourself with the way a highlift jack works. Do the same if the vehicle you have been given has a *winch*. If you get stuck, someone may have the bright idea of using it. How would you feel as their knowledgeable bush guide if you didn't know how it worked? Always have your freewheel hubs locked before a drive.

'Keep it clean'

I was once on safari in the Serengeti in an extremely wet year. It was so wet, that on arrival at the Seronera airstrip, only the windsock was there to welcome us. No vehicle was there to meet us, as flooded rivers had blocked all traffic. Eventually our local Tanzanian guide arrived. He was freelancing for the safari operator who was outfitting our safari. We set off on safari, but it wasn't long before we were well and truly stuck in a muddy bog, with the vehicle leaning at a very acute angle. When we asked our driver/guide if he had a winch, he replied in the negative. We began collecting rocks and branches to insert under the wheels. We dug under the chassis and wheels and generally had a great time getting covered in mud. One of us went to inspect the front of the vehicle to see how much progress we had made, and there, behind the front bumper and under the toolbox, was a winch. Imagine how embarrassed you would feel if you didn't even know that you had a winch on board your own vehicle?

- Make sure there is a **wheel spanner** that fits **all** your wheel nuts. A number of old vehicles with 'character' will have had some interesting bush repairs done to them during their long and hard lives. When changing a flat tyre, having loosened four of the wheel nuts with the standard wheel spanner, a surprise may await you, the fifth nut being of a different size. You would look quite silly trying to take it off with your Leatherman tool.

  If you had something as common and simple to change as a flat tyre, but your spare was flat, or you had no wheel spanner, you would be stranded for quite some time. Because of this basic oversight you would be wasting your clients' precious safari time. It would not help you to string out a list of feeble excuses blaming everyone else but yourself.

'The most profitless thing to manufacture is an excuse'

Even if you do accept the blame, it would not bring back the wasted hours they spent at the roadside.

If an unplanned situation does arise, (which occurs with great regularity because of the beating the equipment takes in a harsh and demanding environment), and you have all of the above-mentioned tools and know how to use them, you will look that much more professional and the safari can get underway again without much time having been lost. It may sound like a lot to prepare, but once you have all the equipment in your vehicle, it only requires a five-minute check before you go out.

- A few *beanbags* add a professional touch for the serious photographer, who will be glad to rest a large lens on one to stop camera shake when the vehicle is stationary and switched off.
- *Wet wipes, suntan cream* and *insect sprays* are always much appreciated at the opportune time.
- Always pack a *cooler box* with drinks and ice. Ask your clients beforehand what their drink preferences are and pack accordingly. Throw in a few 'munchies' and pass them around at a drinks stop - they are often not expected and much appreciated. If you happen to encounter an incredible wildlife spectacle, your enthusiastic clients may want to spend the whole day enjoying this once-in-a-lifetime opportunity. Make it more enjoyable for them by having a good supply of emergency snacks. Always be prepared to spend an entire day out if the need arises, so have sufficient drinks, water and food. Ensure that you have sealed bottled water available.

Bottled Water

These days many visitors from First World countries won't drink any kind of water that is not from a sealed bottle. No matter how pure and clean you may tell them that your borehole water is, they will often be uncomfortable with it. Don't force them to drink it. If they do drink it under duress and come down with a debilitating stomach bug (which may have come from the last camp they visited, or from this morning's breakfast), the first thing to be blamed will be the water that you made them drink. Their stomach bug may have them bedridden for a number of days. They could put the blame on you.

While paddling down the Zambezi River on a canoe safari a few years ago, an American client asked the guide for some bottled water. This guide didn't understand the needs and fears of folk from the First World. He told her there was no bottled water and that she should drink from the river. When she expressed concern as to its cleanliness with hundreds of hippo around, he said to her "you won't die if you drink it". The next day we had to fly the client and her friend out from the canoe safari because the water question wasn't handled in the correct manner, and we had to book them into another safari camp.

These clients came from one of our most productive international suppliers. On their return to America, the clients demanded a refund for the canoe safari because of the way the guide had handled the water incident. We refunded the whole amount for the canoe safari, paid for the unscheduled air charter and for the accommodation at the alternative safari camp. This little incident cost more than US$3 000, all because of a drink of water, and a lack of tact and understanding.

On a number of occasions I have seen visitors holding the bottled water up to the light to see if any foreign items were floating around inside the bottle. They have also studied the top to see if it was sealed. Times and tourism are changing, and if you are offering a service to international clients and charge international prices, they will expect to be given bottled water. Most of these expectations however are not too difficult to meet.

Swing the starter of your vehicle to make sure your battery is strong. If so, you are ready for your game drive!

'Who needs bottled water?'

Chapter 6

Gamedrive

'Take your eyes off your watch and watch with your eyes'

Time

As guides we are always trying to make our clients slow down and steer away from the commands of the little machine that is worn on the left wrist, which controls so many lives. Many guests come from fast, First World lifestyles, where everything revolves around a race against time. It is so rewarding to watch these people slowly relax and unwind as their body clocks adapt to African time.

Just because the clients are trying to slow down and have a relaxing holiday, doesn't mean that you can do the same. *You* are working, *they* are on holiday. While they appreciate time spent unwinding around the campfire in the evening or watching the camp waterhole after lunch, they fully expect the safari activity to leave at the stipulated time. If a departure time is agreed on, make sure you are fully prepared and ready at least fifteen minutes before that time. You will then be in a relaxed state of mind and ready to use your senses and present the wilderness to them. If you are still racing around, cleaning your vehicle, filling cooler boxes, taking a last-minute shower and getting dressed on the run, there is a good chance that you will have forgotten something of vital importance (see the previous chapter). You will not be in the right frame of mind to go out there, find and show the wildlife that your clients so eagerly want to watch and experience.

Wasting Time

If afternoon tea is set for 15:30 and guests have been told that the game drive departs at 16:00, make sure you are not the reason that everyone is still at the tea table at 16:15. Don't dilly-dally around the tea table wasting precious game-viewing time with idle chatter and worthless banter. Must eager guests stand around while the guide pours his third cup of tea? This practice is often used to waste time so that the game drive time is cut short. If you are meant to be out there watching animals at 16:00, then stick to it; don't short-change the clients who are rearing to go because you have lost the enthusiasm and interest you once had.

Introductions

If you haven't met the people you are about to take out on safari, introduce yourself, shake their hands, look them in the eye, and most important of all, **memorise their names**. The ability to remember names is one of the best attributes one can develop in the tourist industry. Guests are always appreciative if you remember their names, especially since hundreds of names go through safari camps each year. If you remember their names, they won't feel like just a number in the sausage factory.

If you know most of the people in the group and they are joined by a few new guests, introduce them, and make them all feel relaxed. Treat them as you would guests in your home, because that is what your safari camp is, your home and your clients, who are your guests.

Tell them if it is going to be cold, hot or wet, and if some don't have the appropriate clothing, suggest they go back to their rooms and collect the relevant items. The short time this will take will far outweigh the sunburn, cold or discomfort from which they may suffer later on.

'Who's for another cup?'

Where to Seat Everyone

Analyse your group as best you can, look and see who has a lot of photographic equipment, who is old or handicapped, and place them accordingly in your vehicle.

Help people up into the vehicle, warn them to mind their heads on the roll bars, make sure everyone is comfortable and have all they need. If one of the party always likes to be in the limelight, don't put him or her in the seat next to you as that person will attempt to hog the conversation, dominate the drive and spoil the experience for the others.

Briefing and Special Interests

Before rushing off to be the first vehicle in line to find the animals, spend a few minutes describing the area, inform your clients what you are planning to do, where you hope to go and what you expect to find in that area. Ask if anyone has a special interest, be it birds, butterflies, photography or a certain mammal. Get a feel for what they would like to see and what they may have seen already. Let them know that you will try to find and show them as much as possible, but that nothing is guaranteed in a wild and unprogrammed situation.

Should you follow up on the special interest requested, don't let it dominate the game drive; an outing is not meant to please only one person.

Smoking

As a guide, you should refrain from smoking at all times while conducting a safari of any kind and in the company of guests. Have a sign in your vehicle requesting guests not to smoke. Smoking has become a social taboo in a number of First World countries. The last thing people expect is their guide to show them the wonders of the natural wilderness with a cigarette dangling from his mouth, puffing smoke all around the vehicle.

How to Drive

A high percentage of your visitors will have come from the 'rat race' where everyone competes in the fast lane. They want a total break from that existence. Drive *slowly* so that you do not miss the animals they have come so far to see. Fast driving, too, can kill birds that don't have the time to take off from the road on which they have been feeding. Don't chase after animals with your vehicle. If a chameleon or tortoise crosses the road, stop and give it the right of way. Once it has crossed, if you don't think you will overstress the animal, pick it up and give your passengers a close-up view while describing its interesting features.

Don't be in a rush as you guide. If you see the spoor of a lion, leopard, hyena, rhino, elephant or other interesting signs on the side of the road, stop your vehicle and reverse. Alight and point out the various aspects of the print. All tracks have a story to tell. Point out these small things while you drive, as your clients will realise that you have an interest in what you do and that you are not only looking out for the big animals. While pointing out the tracks and signs, make sure your explanations don't dominate the drive.

If you must drive faster than normal, apologise and let them know why. It may be because you have to be out of the park by a certain time, or your guiding may have been so productive that you may be late leaving the park. Someone may have radioed you about an unusual animal sighting. You would like your clients to see it, so explain how far it is, how long it should take you and excuse yourself for driving faster than you normally would.

Speed

There is never a reason to speed and endanger life or limb. You may think you know the roads well, or can handle your vehicle on all types of terrain, but you can't predict when another vehicle may come in the opposite direction on a windy bush road. There can be no excuse for a head-on collision when you are meant to be pottering along on a game drive looking for animals.

While on safari in the Okavango Delta with a group of fellow tour operators and a photo journalist, we were making our way back to camp in mid-afternoon, having been out for the whole day. The photojournalist informed our guide that he had misplaced his expensive light metre. He thought it might be at a picnic site some 20 kilometres away. This site happened to be in the opposite direction to where we were going. We were all happy to go back and look for his light metre. Our young guide, who up to this point had been informative and amenable to most things, then showed his immaturity in handling the situation. He drove off in an obviously foul mood, speeding and swerving like a maniac. We told him the light metre wasn't worth us having an accident and causing possible injury. We were unfazed at the time lost, as we had seen so much that day.

Such a display of terrible driving and ill-temper, all for the sake of an hour lost! Imagine the time lost and hospital time if he had rolled the vehicle, or hit one of the many massive Mopane trees that lined the narrow road. We didn't find the light metre, and drove back at a normal speed and still arrived in camp before sunset, so what was all the fuss about? An interrupted and disturbed routine? Insecurity and immaturity? Burnout?

None of these was worth the tantrum, speed and combined displeasure at the scenario in which we were suddenly caught up, with our lives in the hands of a guide who couldn't handle a little pressure.

It is always possible to hit a stump, bump, heavy corrugations, an erosion gully, sand or mud on the road, and that your vehicle will veer off the road and have an argument with a 300 year old teak, mopane or leadwood tree. Accidents through speeding can cause injury to clients and damage to their equipment, and you alone will be blamed. An accident can result in severe pain, hospitalisation, loss of safari days and holidays, no camera or binoculars for the remainder of the safari, and lengthy court cases for the safari company for which you work. It isn't worth it, no matter how late you will be and how much trouble you will get into. ***Don't speed!***

A freelance guide was working for one of the safari operators in the Matobo National Park. The guide, who was new to the park, was driving along thinking more about a big tip at the end of the safari than the big speed hump which lay in ambush ahead. He braked, but too late. While some of the guests were launched into the front seat next to him from the middle tier of seats, the other guests took the brunt of the whiplash effect as the back wheels parted company with terra firma over a mountain of a hump. The two Americans in the back seat were projected skywards, made contact with the steel roll bars, and then fell into the vehicle in a very sad state. The American woman was most upset because of a painful coccyx, three chipped teeth that required capping, and a numb jaw.

Two days after the guests had departed, the dreaded fax arrived, asking for an outlandish amount of money, or else! The next six months were involved in communications with American lawyers. The case was eventually settled out of court.

The freelance guide went off into the sunset, minus his tip and minus the prospect of ever being re-employed by that particular lodge again.

Drive ***comfortably***. Your clients don't have a steering wheel to hold on to while you career around bush roads at high speed. Think especially of those in the back seat, over the rear wheels. This is a very bouncy place to sit. If the road is bad, go into low range and chug along at a snail's pace. A lot of safari goers are elderly; they don't like being bumped and thrown around.

Drive *carefully*. If you go off the road, try not to drive over spiny branches, as it may cause a puncture. When off road, be mindful of antbear holes. If your front wheel drops into one of these, the vehicle can come to an instant halt, throwing its occupants into the roll bars or dashboard. Always inform your clients of overhanging branches, as they may harm an eye, tear flesh or clothing. Be especially aware of these obstacles at night when driving with a spotlight, because they are often invisible to the people in the back because of the dark night and the bright light. We don't need to go into the consequences of injury resulting from irresponsible driving. Apart from the pain and suffering, they are blatantly obvious in a litigious world. Careful driving extends the life of the vehicle. Your employers will expect you to look after their valuable assets.

Be *considerate*. Be mindful of dust whenever you stop; realise that your vehicles' dust trail will curl over your passengers from behind. They won't enjoy it; neither will their cameras and binoculars. If another vehicle is stationary and its occupants are watching wildlife, don't shower them in dust as you drive past at 80 kilometres an hour. You have the name of your company to uphold.

Drive *wisely*. Don't take risks. Discretion is the better part of valour. When you come to an obstacle, evaluate it very carefully. Don't let your youthful enthusiasm make you do a foolish thing that will cost time, an injury and possibly an overnight stay in the vehicle. These obstacles are usually high water, muddy crossings, steep riverbanks or loose, sandy rivers. As keen as you may be to take your clients to

'Go slow Seymour'

see a certain thing on the other side of the obstacle think about the consequences if you don't make it. Often people will be polite and understanding and make the most of the adventure of freeing the vehicle from foul smelling, sticky mud, but how much game viewing time will you have lost by taking this risk? Before VHF radios were commonplace, a number of nights were spent in the vehicle with no food or blankets, because the guide took an unnecessary risk and got stuck. But the clients had paid big money for the comfort of an upmarket safari camp. Unfortunately, it takes a few incidences from the school of hard knocks to learn this lesson.

Be *observant* in your driving. While looking out for animals and birds, read the terrain in front of you: prepare for bumps, humps, badly cambered corners and anything else that will make the journey uncomfortable.

Many years ago, a young guide took a family of five Americans into Hwange National Park. He is a very keen and enthusiastic person. He had driven a lot further into the park than most guides from the same safari company ever did. He hadn't told anyone where he was going and in those days VHF radios were almost unheard of in Zimbabwe. They sat at a waterhole enjoying the sunset and all its natural visitors until dusk. He then reversed the vehicle away from the waterhole, oblivious of an old unused concrete water trough, about a metre deep, behind the vehicle. He reversed into it, the vehicle rolled over, one of the children hurt an arm and the occupants were all quite shaken. Fortunately, the water pump attendants came over and helped them to right the vehicle, thereby saving them a night at the waterhole. Not the situation any guide would like to be in with a group of scared and displaced clients!

Be *informative* about the terrain. Explain that you are coming to some elephant potholes in the road, so your passengers are prepared for some discomfort as you slowly negotiate them. When about to drive through a dry river bed, tell your guests to hold on as you descend the steep side of the bank and then race across the loose sand. If passengers are unaware that they should hold on, they may hurt themselves. If you need them to get out and assist in helping the vehicle across with a push, or if you get stuck, always check that the surrounding area is free of lion, old buffalo bulls or cow elephants before your guests eagerly go off in search of logs and rocks to put under the stranded vehicle.

If you see *litter* on the road or its verges, stop and pick it up. It is the least your guests would expect of you as a conservationist. Ask your guests to keep all their litter **in** the vehicle. People often think it is all right to throw out biodegradable fruit. In the time it takes to break down, how many people will have had to drive or walk past the exotic orange peel? These things do not belong in a natural environment. Ask your guests not to throw cigarette ends into the bush, lake or river. Some go to the extent of burying them a few centimetres into the ground. With a little wind or animal digging, they are soon exposed. The cork in the filter takes a long time to break down. Never allow any foreign matter to be discarded into such a pristine area.

I was a guest in a new, upmarket safari lodge whose 'mission statement' revolved around conservation, conservation, and more conservation. We were due to go out on a game drive at 05:30. A very pleasant Belgian couple and I had tea together around the fire as dawn broke. Our guide arrived late at 05:45 without an excuse. He certainly was dressed the part. Despite being in the middle of a very big camp complex, he had his rifle over his shoulder, sunglasses on (even though the sun hadn't yet risen), his short shorts were rolled up, his jacket collar was turned up in the latest 'model' position. His jacket sleeves were rolled up to expose a number of elephant hair bangles. In a very rugged and cool voice he beckoned us to his safari vehicle.

I had been informed the previous day about the strict training course that these guides all went on. Part of this was about tracker/guide relationships. At this camp the trackers sat on the front left fender of the safari vehicle in a specially designed seat. When we arrived at the vehicle; neither the guide nor the tracker greeted each other, neither were we introduced. It appeared they were both still trying to wake up.

Off we drove, feeling like we had inconvenienced our guide by getting him up at such an early hour. We passed a small herd of waterbuck standing in the woodland with neither our guide nor tracker taking notice. The Belgian lady eagerly pointed to the animals as we went racing past, but the guide and tracker didn't observe her actions either. Not much further down the road we drove past a herd of eight old male buffalo. Once again none of our dedicated rangers were aware of these until the Belgian lady let out a shriek of delight, while pointing to the herd now well behind us. Our steely-eyed guide jammed on the brakes, enveloping us in a morning talcum dust bath. He slammed the vehicle into reverse, and accelerated at high speed to the old dagga boys, proclaiming "buffalo"! We were very pleased to be informed of the species!

A little while later, as we continued on our silent journey, he hadn't said anything other than "buffalo" since leaving camp. I spotted something white in the road. As we drew nearer I saw it was an empty plastic milk bottle. I thought to myself, he will definitely stop to pick this up. No such luck. We sped on and over it, making a popping sound as one of the rear wheels crushed it. Soon after this, the radio came to life and we were informed of a cheetah sighting some distance away. So back down the road we raced, over the squashed plastic milk bottle once more and on to the cheetah sighting. It was the kind of sighting which took the Belgian gentleman nearly five minutes to see the cheetah; nevertheless, it was good to see such a rare cat. Having spent about 15 minutes looking at the cheetah, our guide radioed camp and informed them that we would be arriving for breakfast in figures, one zero (10 minutes). Did we have any special requests for our breakfast order? Well yes, another two hours of driving around in the bush would do, I thought. We drove over the milk bottle for the third time and arrived in camp at 07:30.

Would you have put your name to this game drive? Our guide had totally missed the point; we couldn't really care what our breakfast was like. The Belgians had flown thousands of kilometres to see wildlife, never mind breakfast. Within the first minute of meeting him, we could see he was totally disinterested in his job, and in all his surroundings. The Belgians flew out of the international airport at midday. That was the last game drive of their safari holiday. What a send off! What a way to remember a safari holiday!

'Live to observe'

Off Road Driving

As a guide you are under pressure to 'present' and 'satisfy'. The guest desires the type of results the brochure has promised and about which they may have fantasized. There are a number of safari camps in Africa that do not allow off road driving. This may be attributable to their ecological management plan, company policy or National Park regulations. The temptation, however, when watching a pride of lion through your binoculars as they lazily rest beneath a tree 100 metres away, to 'bundu bash' right up to them, possibly giving your guests the highlight of their safari, is very strong. You recognize, with frustration, how appreciative they would be for manoeuvring them into this exceptional position, thus enabling them to photograph and savour such an experience. Isn't that what guiding is all about, pleasing the guest? Without a doubt! But not at the expense of harming the habitat or earning a fine from National Parks as this could put you or the company for which you work in dubious repute. An accumulation of these offences could jeopardise the renewal of the lease for the safari concession your company has contracted with the Department of National Parks and could also impact your standing as a guide.

If you are on a private safari concession and the owners and directors have a policy prohibiting off road driving, respect it. This rule will have been implemented for a number of reasons like poor grass cover, fragile soils, too many vehicles using the concession to sustain any off road driving, and sensitivity towards mammals, birds and reptiles. It is extremely unsightly to see a maze of vehicle tracks covering natural areas of barren soil or grassland.

Should you work in an area that allows off road driving, consider yourself fortunate. Always remain respectful of the privacy of various animals, the habitat across which you drive, ground nesting birds and the vegetation. Whenever approaching any form of wildlife, don't get 'in their face' by obtrusively imposing into their social life. Approach with sensitivity, as slowly and quietly as possible. Let them get used to your presence. There is an ever-increasing trend towards safari visitors wanting to view wildlife in its most natural and undisturbed state. If your approach results in the animal or herd having to run away, this type of guest will feel uncomfortable and unhappy at the forced human disturbance. Isn't that why wildlife sanctuaries have been created, to let these spectacular species live in peace after so many centuries of human interference? Your persistent presence off road at the site of a lion lair or leopard kill may compromise the survival of the particular animal. Hyena, for example, investigate disturbance in their territories and will find lion cubs sooner once vegetation has been flattened by vehicle pressure. The leopard you are viewing may lose its kill to a hyena and, while you and your ecstatic guests may have had a spectacular sighting, you might want to think about exactly what caused the interaction you have been 'privileged' enough to witness. Roads or tracks that form into a hyena or wild dog den only invite investigation by other predators with undesirable and sometimes disastrous results. These guests know that a great deal of environmental damage or scarring is taking place under the tyres of the vehicle.

Some people dislike the bumpy bouncing caused by off road driving, but don't comment because they feel their guide is determined to do his utmost to produce the goods. Others won't express their displeasure in driving off road; they simply won't come back to your operation and will tell their friends not to either.

Even if off-road driving is allowed and encouraged by the safari camp, be ever conscious of environmental damage. Driving off road in the middle of winter when the grasses are at their driest could cause your tracks to be seen by all who travel down that road in the coming months. Driving off road in the middle of summer when some areas are water logged can be even more damaging and leaves tyre ruts that certainly don't disappear in the next summer or even the summer after. These ruts can cause excess runoff by channeling rainfall and may result in the desiccation of seep lines that would have provided important dry season grazing, they may destroy the crust of extremely sensitive sodic soils and result in sheet and scarp erosion on these important sites. In some areas, off road driving could leave tracks that will scar the landscape for up to 100 years, for example: the sensitive plains of the Namib Desert, Skeleton Coast and the Kaokoveld. Don't ever go off the tracks and roads in these regions!

In some areas there may be animal dens hidden in the grasses. Drive unknowingly into an ant bear hole and your vehicle will come to an immediate and jarring halt, with the possibility of your passengers' teeth being embedded in the dashboard or perhaps a leg, knee or rib injury caused by people being thrown against the bodywork of the vehicle. This could turn out to be a painful event for someone and possibly ruin the rest of his or her holiday. Your company might receive a nasty lawyer's demand a month or two down the line. Why risk it? If you are allowed to drive off road, do so only when you know that you have a rare or important sighting that will significantly enhance your guests' safari and never at the expense of those creatures and their ecosystem you are trying to protect. It is worth remembering that the animals you are viewing are only there because of the continued existence of their particular habitats. Damage these and you ultimately damage the chances of survival of the very species and individual you have gone to so much trouble to view.

Switch Off

Whenever you stop to look at anything, switch your engine off. The noise of a running motor while you are watching a wildlife drama is noisy and distracting, not to mention all the unpleasant fumes that fill the air and engulf everyone's nostrils. It is difficult to look through binoculars while an engine is ticking over. It is also almost impossible to take a photo with a big lens from an idling engine.

While peacefully sitting and watching a pride of lion or a herd of elephant entertaining you with their social behaviour, having another vehicle drive up to share the scene but without switching off their engine is one of the most irritating things with which a guide can be faced. A noisy engine accompanied by even louder occupants of that vehicle emitting loud streams of meaningless comments like "here kitty, kitty, here pussy, pussy", is often enough to make one drive off in disgust.

Discipline

When you arrive at your client's first lion sighting, they will be bursting out of their skins with excitement. If there are other vehicles watching the same setting, you should respect their privacy and enjoyment. As you drive up, ask your clients politely and firmly to respect the bush etiquette of keeping quiet while watching animals, especially in the presence of others. If other vehicles are there before you, don't manoeuvre your vehicle into the best position, thereby blocking off the view of the others. Most of all, respect the animal, don't abuse its space. A cheetah may have worked long and hard to make its kill, if you pressurise it by driving too close and make excessive noise and movement, it may run off. You will have spoilt a natural event. It might have taken the cheetah two days to eventually make this successful kill.

While in the Okavango Delta with a group of clients, it was our third day and we still hadn't seen any lion. That afternoon our local guide spotted a large pride in the distance. As we drove over to the resting lions, the guests, understandably, became very excited and vocal as they were about to witness their first lion sighting. Before I had a chance to try and stem the volume of the excitement, our driver began to treat them in a military manner and told them to keep quiet in a very loud and tactless way. They were so overjoyed at what they were about to see that they apologised profusely and quieted down as our diesel engine throbbed up to the resting pride. We stopped some five metres away. The clients were ecstatic. But lo and behold, our guide who had just so aggressively disciplined the group, pulled out his radio handset and bellowed into it, calling all the other vehicles to the lion sighting. What a shock for us. We had been severely reprimanded for speaking while the vehicle was making its way to the pride, and now that we had the engine switched off, right next to the lions, our prima donna driver sent radio messages at the top of his voice. Worse was to come. As a result of the radio call we soon had five vehicles around us. We asked him to drive off.

How to Talk

When you drive your vehicle, if you don't turn your head to talk to the passengers in the back, there is very little chance that they will hear what you are saying. This same rule applies if you are guiding from a boat, canoe, on foot or horseback.

When talking to your clients as a group, include each one of them by looking at them individually. Don't look only at the special ones, those with strong and charismatic personalities, or someone whose affection you hope to win. Ask if anyone is hard of hearing, if so place them close to you.

Voice

When you are talking, show some enthusiasm for your subject. You are meant to be doing this job because of a love for wildlife. Care about the environment; speak with feeling and passion. Your clients will expect you to be well versed on conservation topics, so share your opinions and beliefs with them.

When discussing controversial subjects, put forward your views, but don't get over-emotional, especially if some members of your group have different opinions to yours. It's a free world, and people are entitled to their beliefs. Have your say and hear them out, too. If you know your topic and have put it over well, they may eventually change their way of thinking.

Enthusiasm

If you have a good dose of this, you can go a long way in any walk of life. People seek out and are stimulated by the company of someone who is bright, cheery, friendly, happy, energetic, vibrant, uncomplicated and exciting.

The golden rule to enthusiasm is ensuring it is *genuine*. One of the worst types of guide is a *false* one who pretends to be vibrant and excited at everything he sees. Most of your clients come from big cities. They spend their lives rubbing shoulders with their fellow man. They know human behaviour and body language just as well as you are meant to know wild animals. If you put on a false act, they will pick it up immediately and lose all respect for and confidence in you. If you are unable to show emotion, rather keep to the personality that you have than be thought of as a phoney.

Enthusiasm
The real secret of success is enthusiasm.
You can do anything if you have enthusiasm.
Enthusiasm is the yeast that makes your hope rise to the stars.
Enthusiasm is the sparkle in your eye, it is the swing in your gait,
the grip of your hand, the irresistible surge of your will
and your energy to execute your ideas.
Enthusiasts are fighters. They have fortitude, they have staying qualities.
Enthusiasm is at the bottom of all progress.
With it there is accomplishment.
Without it there are only alibis.

Walter Chrysler

Knowledge

Don't worry if you don't have an answer to every question. There is so much to learn, and there is no guide who knows it all (although there are a few who think they do). If you are not sure of something, say so; it costs you nothing, except a little face. (In this industry be prepared to lose a lot of that at times.) Your clients will respect you more if you say that you are 'not sure' or 'don't know' than if you give a made-up answer. If you have made it up, there is a good chance your voice and eyes will have let you down, your clients will know there and then that you are not telling the truth. If you have mastered this unforgivable habit, they may not know in the short term, but you never know who their next guide might be. Another guide may know a great deal about that particular subject. How sad it would be for them to find out that you had bulldusted them, and they would wonder what else you told them that was false.

'To talk without thinking is to shoot without aiming'

If you don't know something but promise to look it up when you get back to camp, make sure you do so. I can't stress this point enough. By offering to find out the answer at a later stage is one way of closing the subject, but it will leave a small degree of negativity on the clients' part. If you fail to update them by the time they leave your safari camp, they will know it was to distract them from a topic you didn't know enough about. However, if you approach them some time later with an answer from a reference book, or convey a learned opinion from one of the other guides they will be so pleased that you remembered your offer and took the time and trouble to find the answer. You too, will have learned something new.

You will at times have clients who are more knowledgeable than you are about certain mammals, birds or trees. No problem. Bow to their superior knowledge and learn as much as you can from them. Everyone else will still respect your willingness to learn. You don't have to be perfect. Nobody is. Just try to be genuine.

Positioning

Constantly be aware of how you position your vehicle relative to the animals, a sunset, baobab tree, etc. Remember there are two rows of people sitting behind you, Can everyone see the subject as well as you? When you sight an animal, stop your vehicle and let everyone study the subject through their binoculars. It may run off if you get any closer and at least they will have seen it and will have a good idea of what it looks like. Explain that you are going to try and slowly approach the animal in the hope that it will not run away. Drive a few more metres and then stop. Let them take a few photos while the animal gets used to you. Move on a little closer until you are eventually at a practical distance. If you get too close, the animal may take fright and run off, and you may have spoilt the moment by breaking through that invisible safety zone that all animals have.

'Great sighting?'

You should have at least a basic understanding of photography (see chapter 10) so that you know how to position the vehicle for those who are keen on this frustrating, challenging, creative and rewarding activity. Most clients will have invested quite heavily in photographic equipment and loads of film. Help them get the results they have been fantasising over ever since they decided to go on safari.

Take your own photographs; from the results you will soon know how to position your vehicle for photographers. Your clients will appreciate the fact that you are trying to set them up for an ideal photo. Better still, why not take up photography as a hobby? You live and work in the most perfect environment to pursue such a rewarding interest.

Once you begin to understand the habits, behaviour and signs of the various animals, you will often be able to predict their actions and movements. Use this knowledge to position your vehicle in such a way that their passage soon puts you in the best possible situation for photographic and viewing enjoyment.

Above all, read the animal signals that say, 'don't come any closer'. You may be trying to please your clients by getting them a close-up view of a particular situation. If you disturb the animals natural social behaviour and frighten them, the people you were trying to please will be upset at being the cause of the disturbance. They won't think much of your ethics.

A well-known guide was leading a four-day walking safari in the Zambezi Valley. They encountered a sleeping buffalo. The guests had their cameras ready in eager anticipation. The buffalo continued to sleep. The guide asked them if they would like the buffalo to stand up. In their innocence they said yes, not knowing how he would achieve this feat. He threw a stone at the resting animal, which promptly stood up and charged. The guide shot and killed the buffalo a few metres from his group. You can imagine how frightened, unpleased and disturbed the wide-eyed clients were, not to mention the loss of an animal's life for a photo. It could have ended with a loss of life, or injury, to one of the clients too.

Learn to understand light when positioning your vehicle for a photograph. Africa has such soft light at times; it really can enhance a photograph. Africa can equally have harsh and bright light that can cause photos to come out over-exposed. Your effort and photographic knowledge will save your clients money in wasted photographs, and will hopefully result in some exceptional memories to enjoy at home, either hanging from their wall, placed in albums or used in slide shows.

'That was a bit harsh'

Moving On

Before you start up the vehicle to inch forward to an animal, or when your leave the scene, look around your vehicle to make sure everyone is ready to go. Someone may still be photographing, and your impatience could ruin a picture. If they are still standing in the vehicle and you drive off without warning, they may fall over and hurt themselves, or drop and ruin some valuable camera equipment. Ask if everyone is ready to move. Some may want to stay and soak in more of the moment.

'Ready steady go?'

…en driving around for half an hour without seeing a single animal, …guests informed as to your next plan. At least they will know you are …ing around aimlessly, building up their expectations, only to disappoint …later on.

'Under-promise, over-deliver'

Be Aware

Be aware of the tempo of your group. Don't daydream; your receptors need to be out on stalks all the time. Are the clients bored, tired, thirsty, hungry, hot, cold, scared, sick?

Is there conflict within the group among various personalities? You are their guide, their leader, their protector, the expert on the ground. Most clients are average people, on holiday, and out for a good time. First-timers to Africa often don't know what to expect. You hold that key.

When you pick up indication of discomfort or conflict, take immediate steps to resolve the situation without embarrassing any one in particular. Never say, "because Jane isn't feeling well, we are going back to camp a little early".

Radio-Controlled Guide

Radios are there for emergencies and in the event of unusual wildlife sightings. Find the animals you seek with your own senses, intuition and abilities. Are you a radio-controlled guide, in that you follow all the other guides' sightings from their radio calls? Constant radio interaction is extremely irritating for guests; it is noisy and distracting. Some guides have lengthy radio conversations with their associates (around whom they have been for most of the day). This verbal diarrhoea makes the clients think the guide has lost interest in them and his job.

Avoid slang and code language, as the clients' may suspect you are talking about them in a derogatory manner. If you encounter an incredible sighting, let your guests savour the moment before you call in the other vehicles. Some camps force their guides to identify all sightings to one another by radio. It is a means of showing all their guests a maximum amount of game, but try wherever possible to rely on your own instincts rather than those of others.

Fair Weather Guide?

At certain times of the year guiding becomes a great challenge, especially when the rainy season is well under way, and game viewing is reduced due to thick bush. The animals will be dispersed because of an abundance of water. There may be hard downpours of rain, often just as you want to begin your afternoon game drive. On cold winter mornings the animals will choose the warmth of the forest and not the open vleis and grasslands where you were hoping they would display themselves. This is when your guiding skills will be put to the test. If there is no big game to be found, you will have to create an interest in birds, insects, plants, butterflies, tracks, dung, termites and all the other amazing forms of life the bush has to offer. When game is prolific in the dry season, almost anyone can please a group of tourists - the animals and scenery do most of the work!

The true calibre of a guide is revealed when game levels are low, and weather conditions unfavourable. Incompatibility and strife among the visitors you are taking out may have crept in. These uncommon situations can be caused by the selfishness of some individuals, who always want the best seats in the vehicle, arrive late for game activities and cause delays for others who are yearning to go out and enjoy what they have paid to come half way around the world to see. Tiredness, too, can cause friction and irritability; it often comes about after spending a whole day bumping around in the vehicle looking for animals. Sometimes different nationalities and classes of society can clash. When confined in a vehicle or camp for extended times, your skills as a diplomat and good host will be tested.

Sundowners

Try timing your drive to be at a scenic site or waterhole just before sunset. It gives everyone the opportunity to stretch their legs, relieve aching muscles, mark their territory (loo stop), have a drink and enjoy the sunset and ambiance of an African evening. Avoid popular sites frequented by numerous vehicles and other safari operators, as the feeling of an untamed wilderness will be spoilt. Your clients rub shoulders with millions of people at home; it's the last thing they want to do in an area that is meant to be wild and remote.

'Secret sunsets'

'Nine to Five' Guide

Don't spoil the drive by heading back to camp at breakneck speed. Round the safari off with a slow night drive home. Try to be the last guide back into camp each evening. What is an extra half-hour to your day? By going the extra mile, you may learn something new.

'Take your eyes off your watch and watch with your eyes'

Even though your clients may be tired and dirty, they will appreciate your effort and realise that you are not a 'nine to five guide' who works by the clock and not by desire.

> *I once gave a training course to a group of young and enthusiastic guides, all of whom worked for a very well known professional guide who didn't have the time or desire to educate them. I suggested they should always try to give extra time to their clients by coming back at least half an hour after the specified time. They informed me they would be fined if they came back late because they would be using up too much fuel. Fortunately there are very few other guides and camp owners who have these same selfish, penny-pinching principles. They should be working in the tax department, not in the tourist industry.*

Always leave camp prepared to be out for most of the day. You may encounter a lion, leopard or cheetah kill, have an incredible elephant experience or possibly witness an animal giving birth. Numerous amazing events can occur in the wild. You may have been privileged to see numerous kills in your time as a guide, but your clients haven't. Treat them as if this safari was their first and last time in Africa.

By taking sufficient drinks, bottled water and snacks, you thereby become self-contained, should the occasion arise where you need to stay out and miss breakfast and lunch, possibly even dinner. Regular events like meals should never take preference over unusual wildlife sightings. Radio the camp to say you are going to be late and ask for some food to be kept for the clients' return. Camp staff should understand that things in the wild are unpredictable. They should be extremely flexible regarding mealtimes should the occasion arise, obviously not by inconveniencing any other guests in camp, but by saving some food for your group's return.

With your little stash of snacks and drinks on board, the time spent at an unusual sighting will be that much more memorable and enjoyable. Being prepared can make an enormous difference.

A group of 16 Canadians in Hwange National Park one morning encountered a giraffe giving birth. They were soon joined by a number of vehicles from other safari camps and lodges. All enjoyed this incredible experience. The enthusiastic Canadians made notes and timed various stages in the birth.

At around 09:00, in unorchestrated unison, the drivers of the other vehicles fired up their engines and left the scene. The newborn baby's neck and forelegs were only half way out of the straining mother. They drove back to their respective lodges for breakfast!

The Canadians, who were with a good safari operator, obviously stayed on, witnessing, watching, recording, filming and enjoying such a rare opportunity. They were there when the gangly baby took its first steps in life, and had its first drink from its exhausted mother. What an extreme privilege! Meanwhile, back at the camp all the other tourists were tucking into a standard safari breakfast to which they had been taken back by the disinterested, time-orientated, out-of-touch drivers. It is impossible to call these people guides!

It is surprising there wasn't a mutiny among the guests in the vehicles that departed from this once-in-a-lifetime scene. It just goes to show the control and abuse some guides can exercise over their unknowing and docile clients.

Round it off

On your return to camp, you will often be invited to join your guests for a drink at the bar, or they may ask you to join them for dinner. Don't refuse and scuttle off to your room. Have a drink with them and then excuse yourself for a shower, as your afternoon safari will now have ended. Surely dinner with your clients will be far more stimulating than eating with the same staff who sit and moan about similar things each day? You may have given your guests one of their most memorable days. They want to be your friend; they don't want the relationship to end as soon as you help them alight from the vehicle. They don't want to be just another group of tourists, to be crossed off in the bookings book.

Night Drive

This is one of the most exciting safari activities. There is something special about getting dressed in warm clothes after dinner and venturing off into the dark of an African night. Lions hunting, leopards stalking, hippos grazing, porcupine, aardvark, night ape, spring hare, spiders, mongoose, genets, civets, not to mention polecats, honey badgers, hyenas, jackals, aardwolves, night jars, owls, coursers, dikkops and many more. It presents the opportunity to watch the secretive, lesser known and interesting nocturnal species from behind a powerful spotlight. The diurnal animals are also interesting to observe once night falls and one can see how their behaviour changes. If you have a very strong light, ensure that it has an infrared cover so as not to temporarily blind the animals.

Unfortunately very few camps encourage a lengthy night drive after dinner. It disturbs the routine; the staff want to go to bed after a fifteen-hour day. The guides might have taken three safaris during the day and would rather relax around the campfire after dinner than go out and 'present' once more. Understandably, they are also human.

Bear in mind that night drives are part of the job; think back to how excited you were on your first night drive.

This is possibly the most important time to ensure that you have done all your vehicle and equipment checks, especially your radio. Tell those in camp where you intend going, in case you have a vehicle problem and your radio fails.

Ensure that everyone is warmly dressed. Temperatures differ with habitat. The Kalahari sand regions, being ancient deserts, can be very cold most nights of the year. If guests have gloves and head warmers, they will be of more use to them on their bodies than in their rooms. Ensure there are sufficient blankets. Binoculars should not be forgotten for night drives; encourage your guests to bring theirs along.

Most guides prefer to hold the spotlight while they drive, although it makes driving somewhat more difficult. When you are directly behind the light you will pick up every eye that comes in its beam, even those eyes of small ground-dwelling spiders. You don't have to be rigid in this matter. If there is an enthusiastic youngster on your drive, or an adult whom you know would get a kick out of shining the light, let them enjoy the excitement of spotting some eyes; they will feel like they are helping in part of the show. Try to have all the guests behind the light so it doesn't shine into their eyes on each sweep. If you can, put your windscreen down, so the light doesn't reflect back into everyone's eyes.

Once again, before departing, inform your clients of what they are likely to see, and warn them to look out for overhanging branches and thorns that may catch their clothing, an eye or an ear.

Be mindful of hidden holes and logs when you drive off-road (if you are permitted to) in pursuit of a pair of eyes. When off-road keep a watchful eye on your direction, as it is quite easy to follow an animal in great excitement, only to find that you are not too sure where the road is. Not a great feeling, getting lost at night - let alone the loss of face!

Pan your light across the ground and into the trees for night apes, genets and hopefully, a leopard. Be considerate to the animals. Elephant don't enjoy light directly in their eyes, and impala appear to be blinded if close to your vehicle. When watching a troop of baboons in their roost, ensure you are not directly under them. You will only make this mistake once! The various cats are a pleasure to watch at night with the aid of a spotlight. They appear oblivious to the vehicle and its bright light; they carry on with their nocturnal chores as if you were not there.

Visitors from the northern hemisphere can't get over how beautiful the African sky is and the abundance and clarity of our stars. Always take a little time to switch the vehicle and all lights off to gaze at the black velvet sky, punctuated with millions of sparkling stars. Point out the easily recognisable constellations like the Southern Cross, Orion, the Big Dipper and Scorpio. As you sit there looking up at the night sky, you may hear a variety of night sounds. Inform your clients of their origin. This will help them identify some of the foreign sounds when they are lying in bed each night of their safari.

On some nights you can see many animals, yet on other nights you may encounter very few. However, it's still worth the excitement and prospect of seeing some species that you would not normally see during the day.

Once you get back to camp your guests may be cold. Offer them the opportunity of enjoying the warmth of the campfire and a 'night cap'. Most will go to bed, but those that stay up will often be so overwhelmed by the simple things Africa has to offer that they can't get enough hours in the day to enjoy and absorb it all. It is worthwhile spending time with these people; you then realise how much they are enjoying their safari, and how rewarding your job can be.

'Switch on'

Chapter 7

Walking Safaris

'Your last mistake is your best teacher'

There can be no finer way to enjoy all that the African bush has to offer than on foot. Most guides new to the safari industry yearn for the day when they are qualified to take guests to view all the diverse, intriguing and exciting forms of wildlife on foot.

There are no exhaust fumes, noisy rattles, bumps and engine throbs when experiencing a wild area on foot. An elephant from the safety and elevation of a vehicle is just an elephant. On foot, everyone feels the incredible presence that elephant exude when they cast a wise eye in your now humbled direction. They become proud, domineering, majestic, intriguing, as the playing fields are equalled and you no longer can enjoy the relative safety, protection and means of escape that a vehicle has to offer.

'Equal footing'

There are few means of getting closer and achieving better photographic results of lion on a kill, mating, or with cubs, than from a vehicle. Try approaching as close on foot and you will have your hands full and possibly your guests' trousers too.

In protected areas, wild animals don't associate safari vehicles with death and stress. Vehicles have been around Africa for less than a century. Yet this upright animal that walks on two legs has persecuted nearly every living creature for thousands of years. Watch a baboon mingling at a waterhole among the impala, zebra and sable. It saunters within a metre of an elephant that doesn't give so much as a sideways glance. The baboon crouches down for a drink at the waterhole. Next to the baboon is a Tawny Eagle, also busy scooping up life-giving water. None of the animals is fazed by a baboon - the animal that closely resembles us in southern and central Africa. Sadly, from this beast that walks upright, they now all run, fly, swim, crawl, hop, creep, burrow and slither away from him.

The Joys of Walking in the Bush

Despite this sad fact, there are so many joys to be had when on a walk in a wild area. These include those of walking on a well-used game trail, the smell of dried dung, the plants and flowers, a chorus of birdsong, uninterrupted by vehicle noise, the opportunity to hear the wind move through the trees and rustle their leaves, to feel your skin glow from the warm sun of an early morning, to gauge your direction from the prevailing wind as the hairs on your arms, legs and head quiver in its wake, to feel the gradient of the land from your aching legs, heaving lungs and throbbing heart and to enjoy the health of your body and feel ancient instincts awaken.

While walking you become in participant in the environment and not a spectator from a game-viewing hatch of a mobile metal tomb. You learn to appreciate the taste of warm water from a bottle, which has enjoyed the rhythm of your swinging hips, to bend and weave your way through the thick vegetation of the 'jess bush', to feel the adrenalin burst and rush around your body as an old male buffalo stands up unexpectedly from a deep slumber under a thick bush, while giving you a hungover, antagonistic glare, to watch a lioness' tail whip from side to side as she emits a series of threatening, deep-throated growls, while her cubs scamper around oblivious to your presence, to feel the pain in your neck as you crane it skyward to identify a distant raptor floating high on a thermal. You enjoy the touch of an old rubbing post, the wood and grain of which have been sculptured by years of fire and fine-grained sanding from the sides of numerous elephant, rhino, buffalo and warthog. You learn to sit beneath the canopy of a mahogany, using its broad trunk as a backrest, while being seduced by the bush beneath the cool, deep shade that this evergreen tree offers to all who seek its shelter and comfort, to climb an ancient termite mound, using its elevation as an observation post to look for the lion that you so desperately seek to please your eager guests. This and many other facets are what a walking safari is all about. It is a privilege and a pleasure to be able to walk in a wild area, devoid of roads, vehicles, concrete, power lines and other signs of civilization.

Most guests who come to Africa wish to go on a walk, even if only for some exercise and to get the feel of the land. Walking gives one the opportunity to see and learn about all the little things that we miss when we are in a vehicle, divorced from the land - things of interest: signs, prints, dung, plants and their varied uses.

Read the Book

The bush is like a book where lion, elephant, buffalo, rhino and leopard are the big, bold chapter headings. If you only read the chapter headings of a book you will get the gist of what the book is about, but you will never understand the intricacies of the whole story.

The spoor, dung, plants, insects, birds, flowers, small mammals, butterflies, snakes, rocks, lichens, lizards and many other things are the fine print of the book. If you read all of these you will understand, appreciate and comprehend the 'Book of Nature'.

'Learn to read it all'

When you conduct walks you will be interpreting this comprehensive and most enjoyable book. Just like at school, it takes a long time to learn to read properly. Some people pick up reading with ease, others are plodders. No matter, it is a fascinating, never-ending book. However long you live, you will never finish its contents, nor will you have read the whole story! Most of the guests who come on walks with you will not be well versed in the language of this book. It is up to you to teach, show and interpret its incredible pages, in a safe and honest manner.

You have the opportunity to turn this book either into an unforgettable classic, comic, western, horror story or cheap novel, depending on the way you put your story across. Here are a few hints on how to enjoy and portray this book while on foot.

Types of Walking Safari

There are a number of different kinds of walking safaris. Some cover long distances and include camping at permanent sites along the way. There are also those safaris where the guests carry in backpacks everything they will require for a few days. The most common walks are from safari camps and lodges and take up a part of a morning or afternoon. This chapter will not discuss the different types of walks but will cover the safety factor and basic equipment required.

Qualifications

Throughout the various game-viewing countries of Africa, standards and requirements differ for guides who wish to take guests on walking safaris. I don't wish to qualify the merits of each country and its requirements. There is a school of thought that if you do *not* carry a weapon while conducting a walking safari, you will not take risks by being overconfident from the security that a heavy calibre rifle can offer you. On the other hand, in some countries it is law for guides to carry a heavy calibre rifle when walking guests for hire or reward.

Guides from countries that do not allow weapons to be carried on walks normally support the first mentioned school of thought. They may have a point. Yet at the end of the day it all boils down to the fact that customers pay a considerable amount of money to have a guide walk them in a wild situation among potentially dangerous animals. They put their life and limb in the guide's hands. Are you capable of controlling a situation when a buffalo, wounded in a nearby hunting area or from a foiled lion attack, stands up unexpectedly from a thicket or clump of tall grass five metres from you? Will you feel confident shouting at a ton of enraged beef boring down on you and your clients? What is your plan of action when a tuskless cow elephant decides you and your party are a threat to her young calf? Stand and shout while waving your arms? It might work, but what if it doesn't?

'Hope this works'

It is amazing how forgiving and scared lion, elephant and buffalo are of humans, but there are also times when neither is the case. No matter how good a guide and bushman you are, there are unexpected incidents that arise from time to time and could prove life threatening. Do you have the confidence, experience and resources to protect the life and limb of those people entrusted to you in a situation like this? Will you be able to say that you took every necessary precaution to prevent them going home to their loved ones in a body bag? It's your conscience that you have to live with for the rest of your life.

Most guides believe that you need a heavy calibre rifle to protect your guests. Should an unplanned situation become life threatening, a spear, stick or loud voice is not going to stop a cow elephant with her head down, trunk curled in and ears back, in full charge. As a guide aspiring to take walking trails, you also need exposure with an experienced guide or hunter on how to approach 'dangerous game' and handle tricky situations. Modern tourism is quite different from twenty years ago when almost anyone with a set of khakis, veldskoens and a beat-up Land Rover could pocket the money of unsuspecting tourists and take them on a safari. Modern tourism has many players in the pipeline: the travel agent, the international tour operator and African specialist, the local tour operator and the safari company for whom the guide works or to whom he is contracted. Not forgetting the ever ready and most vigilant predator of all; the lawyer who may make a lot of lives very unpleasant along the tourism pipeline if you have been negligent.

'The ever
ready
scavenger'

Preparation and Training

'Your last mistake is your best teacher'

In most walks of life there is very little to beat practical experience. As mentioned earlier, your best bet is to work for a safe and well respected professional guide. Form a foundation so strong that you can build anything on top of it as the years go by. No matter how tired or busy you are, take every available opportunity to accompany as many experienced guides as possible on foot. Watch how they approach the animal, work with the wind, respect the animal's privacy and read every situation, firstly to the benefit of the animals and then to the client's safety and satisfaction. Walking up to big game isn't about making anyone scared and frightened or getting the ultimate photograph at any cost. It is about respecting the animal's situation, cubs and calves, space and behaviour, watching them in their natural state without intruding on a normal day.

No book can teach you all the animals' footprints, dung, birdcalls, signs or how to track and approach dangerous game. Time on the ground, observing with an open enquiring and uncluttered mind and, whenever possible, in the company of a good teacher, is the best way to learn the art of tracking, approaching and observing animal behaviour. It will take a few years to build up the confidence you need to take guests safely on foot up to the various animals and deal correctly with a situation should things get out of hand.

When that enraged old male buffalo is thundering down on you at full speed with your little band of terrified guests behind you, it helps to know that this is not the first time that you have ever shot a buffalo. That confidence could make all the difference.

'Never forget, it's people's lives with whom you are being entrusted, return them to their loved ones safely!'

During your free time, go out, preferably with one of the local trackers and walk among the animals and learn their ways. Nothing in print can teach you those invaluable lessons!

The following paragraphs assume that you have spent a few years learning wild animal behaviour and are now ready to conduct walking trails.

Guide and Hunter Comparisons

This heading is not to compare who is the 'ruffist, tuffist' and most knowledgeable in the safari industry. These professions are poles apart and they cater for completely different clients. Very few hunters make excellent guides and vice versa (there are some talented exceptions though).

While one profession seeks to satisfy its clients in bagging animals with the largest set of horns, weight of tusk or length of feline pelt, the other caters for people who want to learn the calls of birds and frogs, plants and their uses, animals and their habits. The quest for the ultimate photograph is in the forefront of many non-hunting clients' minds. Their wish to mount the perfect picture, as opposed to the biggest set of tusks, is where they differ in such a big way. The one group can't establish why anyone would want to kill such beautiful creatures merely to adorn their walls. The hunter can't fathom why anyone would want to pursue a butterfly tirelessly in the quest of a photograph. These two groups will continue to misunderstand each other for years to come.

The Hunter

The professional hunter will normally have only one client's needs to fulfil and life to protect. With him will be a good tracker to follow the spoor. Behind the hunter and client will be one or two gun-bearers, armed and often proficient in shooting various forms of wildlife. The object is to track, follow and kill the animal in the most time efficient and humane way possible and preferably without the animal being aware of the hunter's presence. If this is not the case, and the animal flees, the hunter will spend arduous hours pursuing his quarry.

Ideally the animal should be killed with a side-on shot, in the heart, lungs or head, and not normally when in full charge. Should the client miss or wound the animal, the professional hunter's shot is only a split second behind, thus obviating a long and potentially dangerous follow-up of a wounded animal. Apart from the two hunters, the gun bearers will hopefully be on hand to assist with their armory if necessary.

The Guide

Invariably the guide on foot will have a group of up to six clients wishing to see as much of interest as possible and obtain rewarding photographs. They wish to spend time learning and observing the social behaviour of Africa's varied and bizarre animals.

The guide is usually the only person carrying a weapon. He has up to six lives to look after, of all ages, and sizes. A high percentage of clients at the more expensive safari camps are elderly folk from sedentary backgrounds, often slow, unfit, and not used to walking in wild terrain where situations can suddenly change.

The only time the guide will use his or her rifle is when an animal is in full charge and at close quarters, but only after shouting and a warning shot have not had the desired effect of stopping or turning the animal. There is more pressure and a larger degree of difficulty in killing a buffalo in full charge when only metres away, than to killing a trophy animal that will ideally be unaware of the hunter's presence.

For these reasons guides have a difficult role to play in ensuring the safety of their clients. They need to be confident and proficient in handling a life-threatening situation.

'Guide and hunter comparisons'

Requirements

Self-confidence and Assurance
An inner confidence and an affinity to being among wild animals on foot are essential. Even the biggest and best rifle won't be of use to you if you don't have these qualities. Know where and how to kill various dangerous mammals when they are in a full charge.

Rifle
Be familiar and have a sound knowledge and understanding of how your weapon works. You should only own and use a rifle that you trust implicitly; not only does your life depend on it, so too, do a host of others. Bear in mind that a guide will probably very seldom fire his rifle "in anger". When he does, though, it is in a deadly serious situation, and it is imperative that he stops whichever animal at which he is aiming, immediately, either by turning it, paralysing it or killing it stone dead. ***Bear in mind that any rifle is only as good as the handler.*** None of these weapons should be considered a "universal equalizer". The bullet still has to reach a vital spot for it to do its job.

Suggested Calibres

When choosing a rifle, get the maximum knock-down power possible. In most countries the minimum calibre allowed to be carried among dangerous game is .375 inch. This is the rifle with which most young guides first start because of price and their financial situation. As apprentices, they don't earn a lot of money; therefore they can only afford a .375 magnum. At this stage in their guiding career they should be walking around with a .500 double. Unfortunately most guides cannot afford these massive old weapons.

A .375 Holland & Holland Magnum allows for a small margin of error. This is not enough gun for an average guide, who may not be shooting often, and should only be considered by someone who is highly proficient in weapon handling and shot placement. This calibre does not leave as much room for error as some of the heavier bullets. The best calibre rifles that a guide could use are .458, .450 , .416 and .404 magnums, using only solid rounds.

The .458 Winchester Magnum is very popular, and certainly a very capable weapon. Its cartridge received a lot of bad publicity in the past, because it was considered poor ammunition which performed badly. Loaded correctly, however, this calibre is easily capable of stopping anything that a guide may come across. Ballistically, it is not as good as some of the other calibres, as it fires a heavy bullet at a relatively slow velocity. Nowadays, newer cartridges are consistently able to outperform it.

The .416 Remington Magnum is a relative newcomer to the hunting game, but this calibre is proving very popular. It fires a 400 grain bullet at around 2 350 feet per second, delivering effective ballistic performance. It is almost identical ballistically to the .404 Jeffreys as loaded nowadays. Once again, quite adequate for stopping anything a guide may encounter.

The .416 Rigby performs even better than the Remington, firing a 450 grain bullet at around the same velocity. A very good all-round cartridge.

These are the most popular calibres in use today. There are other, larger calibres, which, depending on their ballistic abilities, will do the job better as they get bigger. When considering a rifle, and trying to choose a calibre, ballistic performance should be taken into consideration. Don't forget the saying : **"Use enough gun"**.

Manufacturers

Popular and reliable makes of rifles in circulation are: Winchester, Bruno, Rigby, Remington, Sako, Interarms and F.N. Some of the British rifles are still available by Holland & Holland, Jeffrey, Cogswell and Harrison. Many of the custom manufacturers can deliver models in calibres to suit, if desired.

Very importantly, never assume that a brand-new weapon from the manufacturer is perfect - expect one or two defects somewhere and *check it out very carefully before risking your or your clients' lives in an emergency.*

All of these makes have various idiosyncrasies and similarities, but some important factors to consider are:

- **Action:** It helps to have a heavy action (bolt), with strong extractors.
- **Loading:** Is the receiver wide and easily accessible to facilitate quick reloading?
- **Safety:** Does it have a positive safety action which will not be accidentally knocked off by passing branches?
- **Stock:** Is it adequately pinned to prevent cracking on firing?
- **Magazine capacity:** You need a minimum of a three-round capacity in the magazine.
- **Ammunition:** Is it easily available for your chosen calibre? You will need a lot of it initially while you get used to your firearm, as you will need a great deal of practice.
- **Bullets:** By this we refer to the actual projectile, not the whole cartridge. There is much discussion about the type of bullet to carry, the make, weight, etc. The bottom line is that a guide needs to carry solids, full stop. A good solid will stop an animal sooner than a soft-nosed bullet. A soft nose is sufficient for lion, but will not be any good killing a charging elephant or buffalo. A solid will still knock a lion down.

  There are several good solids available. Possibly the best in terms of penetration are the various monolithic bullets. These are usually turned individually on a lathe, and are made from a single material, usually brass or an alloy. They retain their shape very well, and therefore maintain their weight for the duration of their passage through an animal, and can therefore deliver maximum energy to the animal. Good bonded, full-metal jacket bullets are available now, such as Swift "A-Frame", Trophy Bonded's "Bearclaw", various Barnes solids, Speer's "African Grand Slam", Woodleigh, etc.

  Check to see whether the bullet is bonded or not, and whether the lead core is bonded to the outer jacket. A bonded bullet will retain its weight and shape better than a non-bonded bullet which may break up and reduce penetration and therefore effect.

- **Loaded ammunition.** Many people carry hand-loaded ammunition, as factory ammunition is expensive and sometimes difficult to obtain. Be very sure that whoever loads the ammunition is renowned and has proven over a chronograph that the ammunition is performing satisfactorily. The loader must use reliable powder and primers.

- Always ensure that you carry spare ammunition in a belt or pouch, situated in an easily accessible position. If you have to use more than three rounds and the rest of your ammunition is in your vehicle or at camp, you are not going to look too good trying to cut the throat of an elephant, lying down wounded, with your Swiss army knife.
- Keep your rifle clean at all times; it is your insurance policy. You won't instill any confidence in your clients with a rusted old rifle and tatty gun bag.
- Fire your weapon a number of times each year to ensure there are no faults with the firing pin, magazine spring, and loading. Many lives depend on this.

'I wish I'd cleaned it'

Rifle Etiquette and Safety

Don't wander around camp, in the dining area, bar and lounge like Rambo with your rifle slung over your shoulder. Keep your rifle in its gun bag in camp and ensure it is withdrawn at night from its bag and placed in a discreet, common-sense place so as to allow instant access should the need arise.

If there are children in camp, ensure that they and their parents are fully aware that no one is to touch or go near any weapons. Be especially careful to keep all weapons out of any child's reach. Never go to bed without your rifle. It could be stolen during the night. But more importantly, you don't want to be running around camp looking for your rifle with a client kicking and screaming while being dragged from his or her tent in the middle of the night by a hungry lion.

Never point your rifle at any human for any reason. Ensure that it is never loaded except when walking. Treat this instrument with respect and care; it could save a life someday if used correctly.

'Oh rifle, rifle, where art thou?'

Sidearm/Handgun

A number of professional guides carry heavy calibre revolvers ranging from .357 to .44 magnum. This is a wise back-up policy should your rifle malfunction. A handgun should only be used as a back-up weapon. You could have your rifle knocked out of your hands by a charging animal. The animal could gore or bite you on the ground while your discarded and unwieldy rifle lies a few metres away. A sidearm is useful when canoeing or guiding from horseback, as it is less cumbersome in these situations than a long rifle, even if only to make a noise to scare off a bolshie hippo or inquisitive lion.

The same safety rules apply. Try to wear a sidearm discreetly. Steer away from the Rambo image of packing a sidearm, belt draped in bullets and a nine-inch sheath knife, with a rifle slung over your shoulder while making your way to the camp toilet at midday to adjust your scarlet bandanna.

A hunter in the south east lowveld of Zimbabwe was following up a wounded leopard. He had the misfortune of having this big male leap onto him, knocking him down. It took six revolver shots into the spotted cat's chest before it died. His life was saved by his sidearm.

Bear Bangers and Projectile Flares

These are useful back up accessories to have with a rifle. In most cases all that is needed to stop a charge is a loud noise in the form of a warning shout, shot or dramatic gesticulation. A pencil flare, when fired, will emit a slight bang from the .22 percussion cap, which fires the projectile out from the pencil-like launcher. The flare will light up in the face of a charging animal, and can diffuse the situation if the projectile has been aimed accurately and the distance is right.

I have found bear bangers to be the best of the two projectiles. The same launcher fires out an explosive charge which detonates some 15 metres away, giving off a very loud bang along with a white magnesium flash. This little accessory can be carried around in your top pocket or in a knife pouch on your belt.

A number of years ago while visiting a spring at the foot of the Zambezi escarpment with two good Canadian friends of mine, I was introduced to the efficiency of a bear banger.
We had no weapon with us, as it was private holiday time.

My Canadian friend had shown me his bear banger while we were having our picnic lunch. We then eagerly went to find some of the many lion that inhabit this area.

We found a male lion within minutes and approached him. A large erosion gully lay between us. We didn't see a large pride of females and their cubs lying in the gully and enjoying the shade that it provided from the midday sun. The instant they locked eyes on us, the mothers came bounding up the gully walls, growling and flicking their tails as they menacingly squirmed on their bellies toward us. We walked backwards while facing them, and used our lungs and voices to full effect. Once we had given them a good space, they settled down to angry growls and focused stares.

At this point we noticed that the male lion was no longer under the large shady tree where we had first seen him. We looked around for a few seconds, but he was nowhere in sight. He soon made his presence known in the form of an apparition of flowing mane and bared teeth as he flew towards us in full charge over the edge of the erosion gully, with sound effects and all. The Canadian fired his bear banger. At the small bang of the percussion cap the lion faltered, but soon collected himself and continued on towards us. The explosion of the projectile burst above him with an incredibly loud bang and white flash. He turned tail and fled, much to our great relief. This was proof to us as to the effective use of this little accessory.

Medic's Pack

This subject has been dealt with under game drives in chapter 5, but its importance can't be stressed enough. Possibly, the biggest risk of someone getting hurt when on safari, would be from an animal encounter, while walking amongst dangerous game. Your medic's box is of no use back in your safari vehicle or camp. You need it to be available for instant use, with bandages, drips and painkillers. Full medical requirements for your pack are dealt with in chapter 9.

Make sure you know how to use your drugs and drip. Ensure that nothing has expired or leaked. It is inexcusable to administer expired medication. Check your medic's bag at least once a week. Ensure you are familiar with the whereabouts of all your drugs and dressings and that everything is neat, clean and orderly. Inside your medic's pack always have clean water, a loo roll and matches.

Radio

Test your radio before you leave camp and make sure you have a fully charged spare battery with you. In an emergency a radio will enable you to call in medical air rescue, a vehicle, boat or other form of assistance that can speed up the chance of saving life or limb, your reputation and that of your safari company. All these aspects are closely looked at in a post-accident analysis.

Satellite Phone

I know this may sound over the top but for anyone conducting safaris of lengthy duration into wild and remote areas weather it be on foot, by canoe, horseback, boat or safari vehicle. I strongly recommend including a Sat Phone. Should an accident happen and you have a guest that is severely injured time is often wasted in trying to get communication through hand held radios; comms may be bad at certain times of day or in various habitats.

Messages that are sent by radio often get sent to a number of different people along the chain before getting through to the intended person, during this time your urgent message may become quite distorted and come out quite different to what your original request was intended to be. With a Sat Phone you can speak within minutes directly to the people you need to assist you, weather it be your head office, the medical air rescue organisation, doctor etc.

Sat Phones are also useful when passing on urgent re supply requests when your back up office with the HF radio might have closed down for the day or weekend. In addition for guides who have wives and children whom they might not see for weeks at a time, it is a way of keeping in touch with loved ones periodically. Having a Sat Phone in remote safari camps also has its uses when radio comms are poor or non existent.

However this medium with the outside world should not be abused and used only in appropriate circumstances. Don't forget a Sat Phone is only as good as the battery that powers it; make sure it is charged at all times. This medium is just one more measure to ensure that the guests who are paying large sums of money to put their lives in your hands have a guide with as many safety back-ups as possible.

Maps and Compass

If walking for a long or short duration, carry a map with you, as there is always a chance of getting lost on a cloudy day, no matter how well you may think you know your area. A compass is a small and invaluable tool. People like to look at maps when

at rest to see where they are, how far they have come, where they are going and any interesting features that may lie ahead. It also helps to save face and avert disaster.

GPS (Global Positioning System)

A number of guides use these amazing direction-finding tools these days. It is a good idea to add this to your list of professional accessories. A GPS offers pinpoint accuracy if you are familiar with its functions. You can plot places of interest, eagles' nests, rock art, unusual trees and waterholes and walk directly to them without having to scout around.

The GPS is the modern-day compass, but like all electronic equipment, don't bash it about or allow it to get wet. Always make sure you have a spare set of batteries. Because of the accuracy of this machine, it is easy to become over-reliant on it and ignore your sense of direction. Should the batteries go flat in the middle of a walk, without replacements or you loose all your satellites for some freakish reason or the GPS malfunctions, you could find yourself in an embarrassing position!

Ash Bag

A sock or nylon stocking filled with fine ash is a good tool for testing the wind on your approach to elephant and rhino.

Sunglasses

Once again, this is a personal choice when walking among dangerous animals with clients. For some, sunglasses reduce one's senses and awareness by a small but noticeable margin. When in a tricky situation, which might require well-placed shots to be fired, a pair of sunglasses perched on the end of one's nose may be a hindrance. Some people have sensitive eyes and must wear sunglasses in the severe African glare. The same rule applies to sunglasses as binoculars. Wherever possible, buy the best sunglasses, it is an insurance policy for the protection of your eyes, which are one of your most important senses in guiding and life.

Getting Ready

Numbers

It is inadvisable to walk among dangerous game with more than six people. A group larger than this following you around can become unwieldy, impersonal and unsafe should you walk into a potentially dangerous situation. With a large party the line can become strung out too far behind you to be safe. When you stop to point out something of interest, it can take a while for your group to catch up and share the knowledge you are about to impart. Walking silently in the bush, among animals is a special experience; don't spoil it by taking too many people.

Dress
Before leaving camp, advise your group not to wear white, black or brightly coloured clothing, but especially not white. Although all mammals, except primates, only see in black, white and grey, it is not really bush etiquette to walk in the wilderness dressed like a Christmas tree. Advise everyone to have a hat, comfortable walking shoes and sunscreen.

Safety Talk
You are now ready to commence your walk. You have your backpack with medical supplies, maps, radio, GPS, compass, water, bird identification book, loo roll and matches plus your cleaned rifle and spare ammunition. A few sweets along the way to restore sugar levels will be a welcomed treat. Ask your group to gather round

'No more walk after that safety talk'

for a brief safety talk. There are guides who give a 15-minute safety talk that is so scary, overdone and unnecessary that the whole group is inclined to climb back into the vehicle that brought them to the departure point.

Avoid giving a safety talk that might instil fear in your clients before they have taken a single step. Your guests are on holiday and expect an enjoyable wildlife experience. They are looking forward to you sharing your naturalist talents, not a knee shaker before the walk has begun.

Describe what type of habitat you expect to be walking through, the type of animals, birds, and things of interest you may encounter. To avoid disappointment, don't promise too much. Ask your group to stay close together and behind you and your rifle at all times. Explain to them that should a situation with an animal become touchy, you would like the whole group to remain behind you and with you, not to run away and that your strict instructions must be followed. Emphasize that the walk is not a route march to see how many kilometres can be covered but how much of the area, its pristine beauty, wildlife and signs can be shared and enjoyed.

Ask if anyone has an allergy to bees, pollen, etc. just so you know not to take the risk of showing your group a hollowed-out baobab with a resident beehive in its cylindrical walls. Ask if there are any special interests among the group, i.e., birds, butterflies, plants, etc. Invite them to bring to your attention any mammal or bird that you may not have seen, or to stop you at any time to discuss a plant, skull, dropping or any point of interest that catches their eye. Let them know that it is their holiday and not yours and that they should enjoy it as much as physically and mentally possible. Encourage them to inform you if they are thirsty, tired, feeling sick, etc.

Ensure that your clients fully understand that when you say it is time to leave a certain animal, it means immediately and that there is no time for another photo or video clip. Those few extra seconds can make a lot of difference to an animal that is approaching in a menacing manner. The animal will be that much closer, see your group that much better, and you will be that much deeper into its no-go zone.

Explain what you have in your backpack, mention the medical supplies, maps, water, compass and radio. Do so casually so they don't think you use its contents on every walk. Should something happen, they would be able to use your equipment themselves if necessary. You don't have to explain this to them as it could make them nervous. If during the walk you became incapacitated for whatever reason, your clients could use your radio, medic's pack, map, etc. Always keep written radio instructions on the various channels and call signs in an obvious place.

A *few years ago a professional guide was walking a group of American teenagers (they were in their late teens) down the side of the Zambezi escarpment. It was their first afternoon of a three-day walking safari, which was to end in the valley floor. During the late afternoon the group had a tragic encounter with a breeding herd of elephant and the guide was killed by a cow elephant in front of the group. The traumatised party put the body into a sleeping bag and spent the night in obvious fear of lion, hyena and elephant. The following day the youngsters walked back all the way they had come to find help. Think how a radio, maps etc. could have helped in this stressful situation.*

How to Walk

Everyone joining you on your walk will know how to walk, but not how to get the most out of their walk. Explain to your group that it is normal human behaviour to look down so as not to stumble and fall. Get them to stare at the ground a metre or two in front of them so that they will have an area of about six square metres to look at. Then ask them to lift their heads and see how much more there is to see and appreciate apart from the six square metres surrounding their toes. Encourage them to walk with their heads up for most of the time, and to memorise the terrain in front of them as they take in the scenery from left to right. Once the brain registers an obstacle coming up, it will tell the legs what to do and where to go. There is no need to look down, unless in steep or rocky terrain.

'Look around, not at the ground'

Tell your party how disheartening it is for you as a guide to be walking through incredibly scenic countryside, teeming with wildlife, only to turn your head and see your party trudging along, staring at the heels of the walker in front and missing out on all the amazing sights around them. Explain this in a way that will not make them feel admonished and foolish.

Rifle Precautions

Walking areas differ throughout Africa. Some areas will have lots of wildlife, others will have very few animals. A walk in the latter area will often become a nature walk, where you explain interesting signs along the way. When walking in an area teeming with wildlife, I personally like to have my rifle at the ready, with a round in the chamber. This is, however, a contentious issue within the safari industry.

My main reasons for doing so are as follows: If, for example, you are watching a herd of elephant cows and calves and there isn't a round already in the chamber and soon as the situation begins to get a bit edgy, and you then slap a round into the chamber, just to be on the safe side, the clients immediately realise that things are beginning to change. They think, 'Oh no, he is about to shoot...we are in a dangerous situation...this isn't fun anymore... we don't want to be the cause of an animal's death or put ourselves in danger'! Even though you were only taking a precautionary measure, your action changed their level of enjoyment. Or, you might be the type of guide who likes to make out that every big-game encounter is dangerous and that you are saving the clients' lives at every twist and turn of the game trail.

Should you be walking with your group with no round in the chamber and an old buffalo bull stands up from a clump of grass a few metres away, you would be within his danger zone. His instinct is to protect himself from his biggest enemy and attack. He immediately charges. You shove a round into the chamber and have a bad feed of the round. It is jammed in the breech and you don't have the time to fiddle around and rectify the problem. This shouldn't happen with a good weapon - one you know well and can use, but there is still a margin of error, and these things can happen. There will not be time to sort out the problem. Sloppiness with weapons can be fatal.

With a round in the chamber while you walk, with the safety catch on 'safe', you would always be ready for any occasion. It also makes you very aware of your loaded rifle, where you point it and how you treat it. If you stop for a rest, unload your rifle discreetly. If climbing kopjies and walking through very rocky terrain, again, make your weapon safe in case you fall or drop it.

When walking through patches of thick grass or dense thickets (if you have to), hold your rifle at the ready in case something pops up unexpectedly right in front or beside you. If the situation turns unpleasant and you only have split seconds with which to play, your rifle will be pointing at the ready and you need only slip off your safety catch. You will be in a far better position to protect your guests and yourself than if your rifle was resting on your shoulder or hanging from a rifle sling at your back. Rifle slings are a personal issue. Carrying your rifle in this manner does not give you time to bring it into play should a buffalo, without any warning, come straight out of a thicket at your party. These points are personal and debatable.

Walk and See More

Walking trails offer guides many different opportunities to educate their clients on the secrets of nature, including close-up animal experiences. There is no need to rush a walk. Take your time to enjoy all that is offered along the way, depending on what your clients' desires are. With incredibly keen guests it is quite possible to cover only a thousand metres in two hours. Should you have a group that wants to see as much wildlife as possible, accommodate their wishes too. The walk is not to show off your newfound knowledge and to impress, but to give them a memorable experience.

To Whom To Pay Special Respect

Obviously, all animals should be treated with respect, but some require a different kind of respect. The respect you pay an impala for its lithe beauty and graceful motion is quite different from that for an advancing buffalo bull, head adorned with a large Viking helmet, ready to do battle and chase off intruders that dare to disturb his land.

Below is a selection of a few animals on which to keep a watchful eye. Most of the time these animals will not be a problem if you respect their space. Trouble or injury in the bush is often caused by breaking the rules.

Female Elephant

Cows are extremely protective towards their calves and each other. Single tuskers and tuskless cows seem have a 'chip on the shoulder' and often appear to be rather unpredictable, temperamental and aggressive. The matriarch of a herd will give her life to protect her family if she thinks they are endangered. Elephant living close to hunting areas and in parks that are subject to heavy poaching should be treated with caution. When ambling along, elephant actually cover a lot of ground, so if they are heading in your direction, leave in good time, or they will be upon you before you know it.

The fastest a man can run is 36 kilometres per hour (22 miles per hour). Elephant run at 45 kilometres per hour (28 miles per hour), so don't think you are Ben Johnson. A female elephant can charge with no provocation at all if she thinks her young are in danger and you are too close. A real charge from a cow elephant is quite a fearsome sight, with her head low, ears back, trunk curled in, as her pillar-like legs shuffle at incredible speed towards you. There are more cow elephant incidents with guides in Africa than with any other mammal. Respect these wise and family-orientated animals.

Buffalo Bulls

These old warriors that live in small bachelor groups, or alone, can be quite temperamental at times. If they see you in good time they will normally stand up, advance on you curiously, staring down their raised noses, often turning and loping off after a while. Most unpleasant buffalo incidents that occur while guiding are when walking into a sleeping bull, the whereabouts of which the guide was unaware. Once the animal wakes to see his worst enemy standing only metres away, its instinct for self-preservation takes over and there is a good possibility of a charge. Buffalo that are **not** wounded will sometimes knock the guide over and continue on their way; they do not always stay on to gore and cause havoc. This is generally speaking. Look out for likely places where they may be resting.

Black Rhino

Sadly, due to unscrupulous poaching there are not as many black rhino encounters on foot these days as there were fifteen years ago. These prehistoric-looking beasts give the impression of a crotchety old man who has misplaced his hearing aid and glasses. They are normally encountered in thick bush and the guide can get as big a surprise as the animal when walking into it at close quarters. Oxpeckers are normally a good indicator of black rhino from their scolding chorus as they fly

up in a flock, disturbed by your presence, so take heed of their warning! Withdraw to a safe area as the poor beast stomps and snorts around trying to identify the noise or smell that alerted him to your presence. The rhino will often come past you with a spring in his trot, tail looped over its back and a confused look. If your group is the focus of a charge, this can sometimes be averted by shouting, dodging or climbing a tree. Be careful around these endangered animals; you won't be too popular if you have to shoot one to protect your clients!

Lion

The so-called king of beasts is seldom a serious threat to guides on foot. When surprised, lions often run off emitting a little growl. Mock charges are common if females have cubs close at hand, when a pride is feeding at a kill, or from a male courting a female in season. Their charges have the desired effect on uninvited visitors who may have overstepped the mark by approaching too close. The warning begins with an agitated tail flick from side to side while throaty growls are emitted from a sneering face, with lips lifted and teeth bared. The stiff-legged charge is backed up by snarling and growling, tail erect, and quite a spectacular display of noise and dust. Not many guests want to stay around after such a show. Walk backwards, always facing the cat in question. Keep a vigilant eye out as there are often a number of these social cats together and their camouflage is excellent.

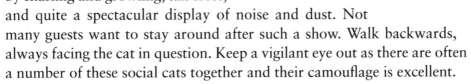

Worth Watching Out For

- Hippo sleeping on land during the day, or when moving from inland water to the river.
- Honey badgers strutting down the same game trail as you.
- Bees and snakes in hollowed out baobabs.
- It is not advisable to stand with your party right in front of an antbear hole; these underground burrows are home to a host of animals.

The wife of a past warden in Mana Pools National Park was knocked over by a warthog that burst out of its burrow. It knocked her legs from under her. She sustained a dislocated shoulder and fractured skull when she fell down onto the hard ground.

A Few Rules

No matter what kind of walk you are about to conduct, there are a few basic ground rules that apply.

• Always go at the pace of the slowest person.

'Go with the slow'

• Never let your group become strung out. Slow down and wait for those that lag behind.
• Analyse your group and walk them accordingly. You don't want to take some blue-rinse old ladies through a jess bush tunnel and then up the side of an escarpment into the middle of a breeding herd of elephant.
• Don't forget most clients want to see maximum wildlife, have an enjoyable time and be safe. Simple enough?

- When you stop to talk about a point of interest, patiently wait for the whole group to arrive before you start your talk. Everyone has paid the same and all want to hear it, not just half of them.
- Walk wisely. Don't take risks to impress. Situations in the wild can change in an instant. Make sure you are never in a position where a finger can be pointed at you afterwards for negligence or inciting undue pressure on an animal. Respect an animal's place in the grand order of things. Don't chase or disturb.
- One of the most rewarding experiences on a walk is to spend half an hour watching a window in the life of a family of elephant with your small group, and then leaving without the elephant knowing you were there.
- Be wide-awake and alert; don't let your guard drop. Pre-empt places of potential danger. Trust your gut! Walk with all your senses finely tuned. You see more, find more and it feels good.
- Ensure that your senses are also tuned in to your clients. Are they bored, tired, thirsty, irritable, sick, and weak? Be considerate of their tempo.
- Never forget the walk is for their enjoyment, not yours. By all means enjoy every waking hour of every working day, but never at your guests' expense.

If you are not legally licensed to walk, don't succumb to the temptation to do so. You may be fortunate most of the time, but not all the time, and when the tables turn, the consequences can be severe.

Six years ago a canoeing guide was asked by his clients to take them walking in Mana Pools National Park. He told them he was not licensed to do so. Eventually they persuaded him to accompany them on a walk. He carried a .44 magnum revolver.

At first the walk went well. Later a breeding herd of elephant walked parallel to the party, but on the opposite side of a gully, apparently quite a distance off. One cow took their wind, peeled away from the herd and came through the gully. The guide fired a warning shot, but she kept coming. The group were hiding behind an acacia tree when one of the party broke cover through fear. The elephant caught her and threw her twice into the air. At this point the guide expended the remainder of the rounds from his handgun into the elephant, which then ran off from the scene.

The sister of the girl had witnessed the whole episode. She was understandably extremely traumatised, not to mention the numerous injuries the victim herself sustained. All because several rules were broken:

The guide had succumbed to tourist pressure and to please them, he escorted the walk illegally.

The weapon he carried was a handgun. It is illegal for a guide to carry only a handgun in an area where dangerous game occurs.

The court case continues as this goes to print.

When walking into a potentially dangerous situation, analyse the lay of the land around you, memorise a fallen tree, termite mound, riverbank, etc.

It is unwise to walk up to dangerous game with no cover to which to retreat, should things become awkward.

When you work in a country where the law requires you to carry a rifle to protect paying guests, make sure you carry it at all times, no matter how short the walk.

During a hunting safari with a very experienced professional hunter, the clients, a man and wife asked to have a break from hunting and to take a few photographs of various animals one afternoon. While driving within the hunting concession, the party encountered a lone bull elephant. The hunter walked the husband and wife towards the elephant to take a photograph, leaving his rifle in the vehicle. The elephant was still quite a distance away when he began to charge for no apparent reason (quite unusual for a male elephant, but possibly caused by living in a hunting area). The elephant knocked over the tree the couple were hiding behind, trapping the wife beneath the tree. The elephant then pulled her out with his trunk and swung her skyward. The professional hunter ran back to the vehicle which was close by and grabbed his rifle. By now the elephant was about to kneel on the woman. A brain shot would have dropped the elephant onto the victim. The hunter shot the elephant in the lungs which caused him to leave the woman and move away, after which the elephant was killed. The wife spent a year in hospital recovering from numerous broken bones, not to mention the trauma of the whole episode. Situations in the wild can turn from peace and sublime beauty to life-threatening chaos in seconds.

When crossing uneven pot-holed ground on foot, tell your followers to be careful and not to twist an ankle. A little incident like this could spoil the rest of their holiday.

Try not to share your knowledge, as if you had eaten English, Latin and Greek dictionaries for breakfast, you may impress a few but not many.

Portray your knowledge in a simple, understandable way: add some humour and a few real-life stories. Make the bush classroom a fun place to be. Don't ask your guests a question about everything that you encounter, often making them look dumb and you, high and mighty when the answer is spewed forth from your learned mouth.

> *While accompanying a guide and his clients on a walk one morning, I noted that whenever we walked up to a tree, he asked the group to identify it. None of them had ever been to Africa before. How were they to know all the trees in the area? Points were awarded to each of the different nationalities each time a question was correctly answered. By all means have fun, but this was the first wildlife walk that any of them had been on, and none of the guests had met each other before the walk. You are dealing with adults. Act like one yourself!*

Make the most of this wonderful privilege afforded you of walking guests in the wild; it is often the highlight of a safari holiday. The whole experience rests in your hands, as well as the opportunity to create the magic and make dreams and fantasies come true. Enjoy it!

'Keep it simple'

Chapter 8

Guiding Principles and Camp Etiquette

'You can't carve out a good career with cutting remarks.'

Ambassador

Never lose sight of the fact that you are an ambassador in a number of different ways. Let's first look at your *country*. Foreign guests often come out to Africa with an open mind. It is so exciting for them to visit a new country or continent and see the sights, but especially to meet the people and see what makes the country tick. There are very few countries in Africa where foreigners will not be welcomed with wide, smiling faces and offered genuine hospitality. Visitors from large, bustling, busy, impersonal and aggressive cities around the world are astounded at the friendliness of the people in Africa. This great continent may not be as fast and efficient as the first world, but that is often the reason people come out to Africa, to slow their pace, unwind and tune in to old instincts.

Most local people the tourist will meet, be they transfer drivers, receptionists, waiters, room cleaners, barmen, gardeners, guides, etc., are extremely proud of their jobs and will be polite and courteous. The last thing the clients want to hear while on holiday is your opinion of how useless the government is, how they are botching up the economy, pillaging the national coffers, steeped in corruption and all the other views you may have of the way things are being politically and economically handled. You work in the tourist industry, therefore you are one of the main ambassadors for your country. You meet far more average citizens from various nations than most officially appointed ambassadors. After all you may be spending days or weeks with Mr Average from a foreign country, rather than exchanging a few polite words at a cocktail party. The way you portray yourself and your attitude towards your fellow countrymen is the impression they will take back home with them. Let it be a positive, happy and memorable one.

Steer away from political discussions. You are a guide, not a politician. There will be a number of guests who will ask your impressions about various contentious political issues. Plead ignorance, or answer their questions diplomatically. Don't be lured into the trap of running down your own country; be proud of who you are and where you come from. All countries have their faults, not only the one you live in. If you can't stop moaning and complaining about your country, go and live somewhere else.

You are also an ambassador of the ***company*** that employs you. During the many hours that you spend with guests they will also question you about the various personalities that own your company, what they are like, their principles and morals. It is not for you to run them down. Don't forget where your salary comes from and who initially employed you. Keep company problems away from all clients. If you are discussing company politics with fellow staff members, ensure that there are no clients within earshot. All safari camps have behind-the-scene problems. They come from being so isolated. Don't involve your guests in them. Always be aware of who is around you when you are discussing in-house problems.

'Mister Ambassador'

If you think the food is bad and the chef useless, or head office is incompetent and the marketing department totally out of touch with things, make it known to the relevant people within your company; don't burden your clients with company politics.

Don't run down and bad-mouth your fellow guides and work associates.

> *'You can't carve out a good career with cutting remarks.'*

In camp life where staff members are around one another for many hours of the day and have no escape from one another, friction and personality conflict can arise. This is a fact of life. Don't bring it out into the open with your clients. If you don't have anything good to say about someone, don't say anything at all. Take a lesson from nature; 'Ears were **not** made to shut, mouths were'.

The Competition

This is another area where you can be drawn in by guests who enquire about fellow safari operators, camps and lodges in your vicinity, or within the country. Ensure you don't bad-mouth them. Either feign ignorance or speak well of them. Many people thrive on scandal; it won't take long before your negative words and opinions get back to the competition. This does not bode well for relationships in rural areas, or between companies in the same industry.

> *'Remember, blowing out another's candle*
> *will not make yours shine any brighter'*

Diplomacy

Be wary when telling jokes to safari guests. Keep *nationalities* out of your jokes wherever possible. Jewish people, Irishmen, the Polacks etc. don't pay all that money to come to Africa on safari to listen to their young host making fun of their nationalities. We are all proud of who we are and where we come from. Don't try and be funny and win favours at someone else's expense. Don't generalise about nationalities and run them down if you think it is safe or funny to do so, especially not when around Americans, as you never know their backgrounds. You may be waxing lyrical about your dislike for Germans and your opinionated views of their bad points; it is possible that one of your American clients had German parents.

Watch what you say about **gender**. Many women these days feel strongly about being treated as second-class citizens and dislike jokes against them. By all means tell jokes at the opportune time, but make sure they won't offend anyone.

When trying to make casual conversation, shy away from asking **pregnant** looking women when their babies are due. I have made this mistake on two occasions, only to be told, rather indignantly, that they were not pregnant. One would have thought that you only make this mistake once in your entire life; obviously some of us take longer to learn life's basic lessons! Guard your comments on religion, gays, old and overweight people.

If one of your clients is being picked on by their family or friends and jokes are being made about them, don't join in, thinking you are gaining acceptance and admiration from their group. The client hasn't flown all this way and paid all this money to be abused by an upstart guide trying to establish confidence in life at their expense. If you see one of your clients being picked on, side with him or her, and help in some way to change the conversation to take the pressure off the person concerned.

'Cork it'

The Social Side to Guiding

Social skills can be a very strong asset that guides can use to ensure their guests have a happy and memorable holiday. Not all clients want to see wildlife fourteen hours of a day. Most visitors are on well-earned holidays and enjoy relaxing at the camp pool, having a beer or glass of wine at lunch, swopping jokes around the campfire, discussing sport, holidays and life in general. If your social skills are used correctly they will go far in ensuring a successful safari.

'At ease!'

Drinking

By all means let your clients have a drink or two during the day, but weigh up their situation. If your guests are staying with you at a safari camp, a few drinks at lunch, followed by an afternoon nap, will do them no harm. If you are leading a canoeing, walking or horse-riding safari, too many drinks at lunch will impair their safety in the afternoon.

Ensure that you don't let a situation get out of hand with one or two guests who become a liability to the safety and enjoyment of the rest of the group. Should your guests have a few drinks in the evening, that's fine, they are on holiday, but the bush doesn't lend itself to wild and noisy parties! Always ensure that other clients will not be disturbed by noise and vulgarity. Keep diplomatic control of the situation. You will also be saving them a sore head, possible injury from a fall, embarrassment and dulled senses the next day.

Have a few drinks yourself in the evening should you wish, but don't overstep the mark. Never lose sight of the fact that you are in a wild area, with wild animals

'No wild parties'

close at hand. Your guests will often be appreciative to you for giving them such a memorable day. As they relax around the camp bar, dinner table and then fireside, they often want to show their gratitude and newly formed friendship to you by sharing a few drinks together. But they don't have your responsibilities nor lives in their hands. You need to have all your senses about you at night. You want to be able to sleep lightly in case there is an incident, or merely to be aware of the night sounds which are always discussed next morning by eager guests.

Be especially alert when camping close to nature. Know exactly where your rifle is at all times; ensure it is always discreetly close at hand. You don't want to be the last one to wake up in camp when a lion or hyena is causing havoc in a client's tent.

A few years ago a small group was camping on safari in a remote area. Once everyone had retired to bed and fallen asleep, a pride of lion came into camp and pulled the young 'gopher' guide from within his open tent. The professional guide woke to his urgent calls and to the sounds of the lion pride. The guide had left his rifle in the safari vehicle which was some distance away. He was unable to get to his rifle and fire warning shots to scare off the lions, thereby possibly saving the young mans life.

Briefing

Clients should be given different briefings during their stay with you. When you collect them from the airstrip, explain the normal drive time back to camp, give a brief introduction to the area, and explain what they are likely to see on the way.

Brief them on standard vehicle etiquette, for example, not to stand up when watching lion, leopard, cheetah and female elephants. Ask them to respect other people in the vehicle who may be taking photos, as unnecessary movement will blur a photograph. Tell them that they should ask you to stop at anything they may find of interest to enquire about or photograph, be it a cloud, gnarled tree, reflection, dung, termite mound, flower, etc.

On arrival at camp, they will be briefed on meal and tea times, camp routine, their rooms and, most of all, camp safety. Each camp has its own set of rules about various four- legged visitors. Ensure that your new arrivals know not to leave their doors or tent flaps open at night.

In the mid-eighties, while overnighting on a canoe safari in the main campsite of Mana Pools National Park, we were awakened at midnight to a lot of shouting from the campsite next to ours. A very nasal voice was yelling the name of their guide. In our group were two surgeons so I went across to see what had happened and to see if there was anything they could do to assist.

It transpired that the client's tent flaps had been left open. During the night a hyena boldly walked into the tent and bit off a sizable part of the client's nose. The tent was in a terrible state; you can not imagine how much blood there is in a nose. There was blood everywhere. The shocked client had defecated in his bed; the hyena had defecated on the floor of the tent. It is not easy to replace a missing nose.

If a lot of potentially dangerous animals frequent the camp area, tell your guests they are not to wander out of the camp boundaries without a guide and should be collected and dropped off at their rooms once nightfall sets in. It is imperative that this briefing is given on arrival. Ask your guests to use flashlights after dark. Explain the safety of the drinking water and point out air horns, bells or whistles in case of emergencies.

Arrange an appropriate time to give your newcomers a short briefing on the area, using a map for orientation. Explain the various safari activities and the time of day when they tend to be at their best. Advise on morning, day and night temperatures, and what clothes to bring on the various activities.

Should they encounter any unfortunate circumstances during their stay, be sure to brief them on those possibilities on day one: tsetse flies, freezing Kalahari mornings with very little wildlife on show; wet and muddy roads due to freak rains; an extremely high flood water in a river or delta (which may also result in muddy bath, basin or pool water). A culling programme may have started, there may be helicopter game counts, a capture operation, or a plague of stinkbugs, corn crickets, gerbils or inchworms. Often, when well prepared for such misfortunes, they can be turned into a fun event.

At each meal, find out from the guests which safari activity they would like to do: hides, fishing, walk, cruise, drive, canoe, rest, etc. Dinner is a good time to advise everyone of the options for the following day. Ensure you put this over clearly and that everyone is in the picture. Make allowances for foreign guests who may not understand English well.

For guides who are about to embark on a prolonged safari of a few days or weeks with the same group, a *thorough* briefing is of utmost importance. This may be a walking, canoeing, rafting, diving, kayaking, cycling, climbing or overland mobile safari. Guests need to be well prepared for the difficulties and hardships they may face and a good briefing will forestall a lot of complaining and disillusionment once the expedition is underway. Such safaris need regular briefings so everyone knows where they are going and what they will be doing the following day. Your briefing could include things like the terrain, the chance of seeing a new species, different tribes, scenery, town or village, border post, etc.

On Guard

When things are going well on a safari and you present your clients with amazing sights and excitement each day, you become their idol, big buddy, fearless leader and hero. You will be showered with praise and invites to come and stay at their homes. Kind and genuine offers will be made to use a vehicle, boat, beach condo, or go on a skiing trip, etc. Don't get too high on the praise and buoyancy of the relationship, it can change in seconds. If you take a risk that backfires, act negligently or have too much to drink and someone gets hurt under these circumstances, your newly found friends who were massaging your ego gland will turn on you in an instant and ensure that you are brought to book for your carelessness.

As mentioned earlier, you may form some life-long relationships with clients, but never lose sight of the fact that first you are meant to be providing a service of many facets. The most important of all is safety. Would you like to dream, fantasise and save for years for a holiday, only to return home minus a limb or a loved one?

> *In the mid-eighties, a canoe party was floating down the Lower Zambezi River. It was a hot day and the guide and clients agreed to float with their life jackets on, next to their canoes to keep cool in the Zambezi! This is a very unwise thing to do in a river which is home to some of Africa's largest crocodile populations. It wasn't long before the obvious happened and a crocodile latched onto the buttocks of a twelve-year-old boy. The boy's father went to the rescue and forced his left arm deep into the croc's mouth. The crocodile spun a few times and swam off with the father's left arm and wristwatch as a meal and memento. The father was left with a stump as a reminder of a careless decision.*

Manners and Etiquette

You may wonder why you, as a double-rugged bush guide, need these. Guiding is a culture and very few guides can compare with the professional guides in Kenya for finesse, turnout and pride in their profession. Guiding is a way of life for most of them; there are often three generations of guides and hunters all from one family. They are proud of their work, understand who the most important person in their industry is and treat him or her accordingly. They are not only well versed in most fields of wildlife; but can discuss at length current affairs, sport, conservation topics and almost any other subject that may be raised while on safari.

Their safaris are often grand affairs with spacious tents, well-designed and comfortable safari vehicles, top-class equipment, excellent food and presentation. These guides are well educated, all speak fluent English and Swahili, have a sound working relationship with their staff and wouldn't swop their lifestyle for anything. They travel to Europe and North America most years to visit past clients and hopefully sign up new ones for the seasons ahead.

Sadly, there are a number of guides in Southern Africa who don't feel the same pride in belonging to the tourist industry. They perceive their job as pandering to the tourist's every whim and need, and often feel lowered by it. Some think a guide should be double-rugged, tough and hard, not showing too much emotion for the animals, scenery and settings they encounter. With such an attitude they won't find happiness and will never be a permanent piece in the jigsaw of tourism.

Eating

A number of basic manners were drummed into us as kids but some of these could fade with age. Don't scoop your food into your mouth from the horizontal level of your plate. Lift your elbows and insert medium-sized portions into your mouth. Chew your food without presenting it for all to see how well you are masticating and the kaleidoscope of shapes and colours. You may think this is exaggerated but it is not uncommon to watch this type of feeding behaviour from guides at some up-market establishments.

Conversation

If you see a guest is being left out of the general conversation, attempt to include and bring that person into the discussion. Pay special attention to the shy, insecure and nervous client. Make that visitor feel wanted and as welcome as the rest of the group. You are everyone's host and guide.

Try and sit with different people at each meal. Don't only socialize and pay special attention to entertaining the high ranking, humorous, good-looking, rich, famous, 'well bred' and titled clients, while shunning the quiet, dull, foreign, fat, old, deformed and ugly.

'Time for everyone'

They have all paid what was asked of them for a safari experience at your camp and with you, so treat them accordingly. Without imposing on their private lives too much, ask about their family, children, siblings, work, home and holidays. Most people enjoy talking about themselves. Encourage them to do so in an unobtrusive manner.

The happy and humorous clients are the easiest to please; any guide can give them a good time. Consider 'difficult' and introverted guests as a challenge to your guiding skills.

Don't sneak off after dinner. If there are other guides in camp to look after the remaining guests and you decide to retire to your home, bid everyone farewell. It is only polite to do so. You may think no one will notice if you simply disappear, but don't fool yourself, they will.

Equal Treatment

During your time as a guide you will have guests who may be staying at your camp either free or at a discounted rate. A couple may have won a prize of a few nights at your lodge. A travel agent or tour operator may be on an educational inspection visit of your property. The company for which you work may have put out a specially discounted rate to local visitors. Treat them *all* the same as the full paying guests. It is not your job to differentiate how guests should be treated. Guide to the best of your ability irrespective of where they come from, who they are or how much they have paid.

'Equal treatment'

Khaki Fever

A subject that we sadly can't avoid mentioning. A number of people who come out to the wilds of Africa from First World developed lifestyles are often overwhelmed by the beauty and vastness of untamed Africa.

For many, some dormant senses come alive and begin to glow for the first time. They begin to enjoy the feeling of space, naturalness, wilderness, lack of pollution, clear skies, warmth, vast herds of beautifully formed animals, refreshing dawn mornings, billowing clouds, electrical storms, sunsets, bird song, the wind, rain and sun on their urban skins. With an awakening of their senses can come an admiration for you, the one whom they perceive has opened all this up to them. The perception that you are in love with nature, so aware, natural, unmaterialistic, uncluttered and uncomplicated also enhances their respect. Some people have never felt the way they do in Africa; free, wild and sensual. This can be the time when 'khaki fever' sets in. They perceive that you, dressed in your khaki clothes, rifle at your side, always a ready smile and understanding your guests' wants and needs are the reason behind this good feeling. There are a number of guides who know this and prey on their guests.

'Beware khaki fever in progress'

It is impossible to denounce bush romances. A high percentage of marriages within the tourist industry emanate from this type of scenario. However, there are a few unwritten rules to observe. If you pick up the green light, ensure that you continue to do your job to the best of your ability. Don't give the person in question any better treatment than the rest of your party, if anything give the others even more attention. You can be assured that they will have picked up the body language from both of you the minute it started. Remember that the other guests have come for a wildlife experience, not to watch the pair of you flirt, giggle and pass private banter. Don't place the object of your newfound lust in the front seat of your vehicle.

Don't try and place yourself at that person's side at each and every meal. Your guests are often well educated, mature and perceptive people who don't enjoy being in the company of someone who is so overwhelmed by flirtatious ego-boosting that he or she neglects their guiding duties. There is nothing worse than watching a love-struck guide bumbling around like a bee to honey, so don't let your instincts brand you! If you have picked up the green light, be extremely discrete and careful. Rather follow up on your instincts during your leave and time off than at your place of work.

If you seem to pick up keen vibes from someone's *spouse*, ignore those signs completely! You are now in very dangerous territory! If you have sensed these indicators, you can be certain that the other spouse has too. Be professional and proud of your work. Keep in the forefront of your mind the reason why you are there. Guiding can be a life-long profession; don't let yourself down.

Tipping

Here we have another difficult and rather awkward area: being offered tips from clients at the end of a safari.

What does **TIP** stand for?

To Insure Promptness.

This used to be an amount paid to a waiter *before* a meal, to ensure that the person who gave the money was well looked after during the meal. In time it changed to an almost universal offering of thanks for a job well done.

There are people such as Americans who tip for every move someone makes, and often for poor or mediocre service. There are those that don't like to tip at all - Australians, New Zealanders and Dutch people come to mind. Irrespective of nationality, you should never *expect* a tip, or be put out if you don't receive one.

You are employed to do a job, and you are paid a negotiated salary. Tips are purely a bonus, should you receive them. If you work towards a bigger tip, you will not be guiding from the heart, but from the pocket and you will never guide well. You will exaggerate and become a bore.

'A tip for the wise'

I have witnessed some sickening tip and gift soliciting from guides. A guide without binoculars or camera might say in front of his clients, "Oh, I wish I had a pair of binoculars or a camera. It would make my job so much easier." A generous guest will feel sorry for the guide, who is a professional at putting on his ' poor little boy look', and at the end of the safari the guide is presented with a pair of binoculars or a camera. Other examples of tip soliciting include film, camera lenses, bird and mammal books, hats, boots, sunglasses, clothes, backpacks, torches, knives, fishing rods and tackle.

If tips for the rest of the staff in camp have been left in your hands by departing clients, don't pocket 80 per cent and give out the balance. It will not take staff long to work out that you are robbing their tip box. If guests want to give you the tip for your staff, rather ask them to present it to them in person. It is these people behind the scenes who are the unsung heroes of the success and smooth running of most camps.

Don't lower yourself and expect tips. You should be proud of what you do and who you are. If guests offer you a tip as a token of their appreciation, accept it modestly and graciously.

Behaviour

When in the company of your guests (and hopefully all forms of man and beast) don't act in an arrogant, conceited, argumentative, self-opinionated, aggressive, selfish or lazy manner. Don't sit at the dining table and 'hold court' as if you were an authority on every topic raised. Let others have their say. Respect their opinions, values and ideas. There are times when a family or friends have come away on a holiday to share quality time together. You must be able to sense this and know when you aren't really wanted around. Don't try to be in the limelight all the time.

Don't take advantage of their easygoing attitude, age, fitness or size. If someone is fat, old or sickly, make a special effort to take that person on a walk, canoe outing or any other suitable activity. Often these kind of folk will come from a sedate, quiet and mundane lifestyle. They will fit into any safari activity without a murmur, even though they secretly would like to join the rest of the group on an adventure.

'In my humble opinion'

Try not to package them into game drives all the time. With a little extra time, effort and attention you could end up giving them the greatest experience of their lives. What a privilege at such a small price. On a number of occasions I have canoed extremely overweight or aged people down the Zambezi. Many of them had never stepped into a canoe before. We have encountered numerous hippo, crocodile basking on the bank, elephant swimming across our bows, a host of colourful aquatic birds lining the banks and shallows; as well as many kinds of antelope, nervously drinking from the river's edge. Where the sandbanks became too shallow, we would disembark and walk in ankle-deep water until it became deep enough again to allow our continued passage. Some of these people hadn't dipped their feet into a river since they were children, let alone into a river like the Zambezi.

At the end of the trip, while we were loading the canoes onto a trailer, it was such a pleasure to see their faces aglow with joy and achievement and to listen to their excited babble as they marvelled at such an experience. For some of these folk the 'hairiest' thing that had ever happened to them was someone's bad driving and poor road manners, possibly by jumping traffic lights and causing a near accident and an adrenalin rush.

You may encounter guests who are frightened of the bush, water, insects, snakes, open spaces, uncivilized situations, wild animals, etc. These fears may have developed because of a terrifying incident in the past, or they may be worried about the safety of their children, grandchildren, spouse, parent or school kids who have been entrusted to their care on the safari. As a guide, try and help them out of their phobia, or be understanding towards their predicament; don't retort with smart or witty comments.

Avoid sarcastic comments. If the game viewing is poor and you are struggling to cough up with the goods and someone comes out with a statement you find excruciating, hold yourself above an immature and sarcastic retort.

I recall, with misgivings, a game drive I conducted one wet March morning while Hwange National Park was in the peak of its rains and there was very little wildlife to be found. I had walked a short distance from the vehicle and was picking a plant to show to the clients. While doing so I overheard one of them say, "We didn't come all this way to see some plant." My hackles rose. I was about to share with them an amazing fact of the plant kingdom from my 'immense store of newfound knowledge'.

While I was walking back to the vehicle, plant in hand, one of them said "There is a lot more game in Kenya than Zimbabwe". At that stage I had never been to Kenya, so didn't realize the tremendous volumes of animals that were available there to please the first-time visitor to Africa. In my youthful immaturity I said to them: "Have you ever been to Amsterdam in winter? If so, you wouldn't have seen any tulips. How can you expect to see masses of animals here in our summer?"

It wasn't their fault that they had been sold a safari to Zimbabwe by their travel agent in the peak of the rains, when game viewing is at its worst. I should have shown an interest in their last safari to Kenya, asked where they went, what they had encountered and learnt something, rather than taking the bait and lowering myself with a sarcastic answer.

Go That Extra Mile

We have already discussed giving more on your safari activity than could reasonably be expected. Extend this attitude to the social life in and around camp. You might be going to check a borehole, tractor grader, labourers, game scouts, the building of a new hide, or take supplies to one of your bush camps. Explain what you are about to do and ask whether any of the camp guests would like to join you. They may not necessarily see a lot of animals, but they will appreciate the invitation and feel special to be included in seeing some of the day-to-day running of a safari operation.

You may strike up a special friendship with some of your guests. Take them to your home, invite them in, introduce them to your wife and children, have tea or a drink with them. They may be keen on natural history books. Show them your collection, or your wildlife paintings and photos. If you have an animal or bird that has been orphaned and you are raising and rehabilitating it, take them to see it. You may own a certain breed of dog in which they are interested. Share it with them. If you are having some local friends around to your house for a braai on your night off and you think there are one or two clients who would enjoy the company, invite them to meet some of the locals and get a good flavour of your country. They will feel they that are not just one of the many standard people in the tourist sausage machine, but extra special people. You obviously can't do this to every client, but give it your best shot. There are a host of things that you can do with guests by giving them that little bit extra.

When I was working in Hwange National Park in the Eighties, steam engines were still a common sight. If I had guests with us for a long time and if I thought they would enjoy the outing, we would drive into the nearby village of Dete, a large railway shunting yard. The engine drivers were always friendly and welcoming to our visitors. They would let the clients come aboard, shovel coal into the furnace, let off steam and blow the whistle. If they were heading down the line to Bulawayo, they would take the clients for a ten-kilometre ride in the caboose, allowing them to assist with all the chores. I would drive ahead and collect them at a railway crossing, where I would always be greeted by beaming sooty faces. Some days we would drop in at the local pub at lunchtime for a beer and sandwich. These little things with the right guests at the right time are some of the aspects that help forge close relationships and bring them back for another safari with you at a later date.

I was once asked by a young and enthusiastic camp manager what he needed to do to win the local award of 'Best Safari Camp'. This award was nominated by a group of local travel agents. I told him that the best award he could wish to win as a camp manager and guide was to have a high percentage of repeat clients! There can be no better accolade in the tourist industry than this.

'Go that extra mile'

Flexibility

In order to guide well you need to be flexible. Wildlife and wild areas are not preprogrammed; if your 'gut feel' tells you to go to another area in your concession while on a safari activity, trust it. Rigidity does not go down well in guiding. In this profession you work with so many different nationalities and personalities that you have to be flexible, to a point, obviously.

While escorting a small group on safari in the Serengeti, we drove between two massive granite whale-back kopjies. It was about 10:00 in the morning. I asked our driver guide if we could climb one of the kopjies with our picnic basket for tea. He had been driving since sunrise and was obviously well embedded, deep down in his seat. He said, no, we couldn't.

To be in this particular area of the park we had to have a National Parks game scout with us. Refusing to be put off by the driver, I asked the game scout if we could climb the kopjie. He said it wouldn't be a problem. I relayed this to our driver who then had no option but to stop.

We climbed this great whale-back. What a view greeted us on the summit. A green basin of grass, thousands of hectares in size, filled with over a thousand zebra. What a sight to see so many of Africa's black-and-white horses, peacefully grazing below us. It was an incredible setting. We sat on the colourful lichens of the granite, sipping tea and crunching on rusks, our binoculars often fixed to our eyes, scanning the scene below us. Soon we spotted a small group of hyena, then three cheetah, only their heads visible above the lush green grass. We sat up there for over an hour, absorbing one of the finest views on earth.

On the last evening of this four-week safari I asked our small group what the highlight of their safari had been. We had enjoyed the Serengeti wildebeest migration, surely one of the world's greatest wildlife spectacles. We had seen the Ngorongoro Crater, the chimpanzees of the Mahale Mountains National Park on the unspoilt shores of Lake Tanganika, and 'Selous', the world's largest game reserve. We had been to the historic and colourful town of Zanzibar, and had enjoyed scuba diving off a pristine island in the Indian Ocean, over untouched coral reefs.

Their unanimous highlight? 'Sitting on the kopjie, with a thousand zebra knee-deep in life-giving grasses below us' they said. We could have been robbed of this experience had we not had that flexible game scout with us, robbed of what was to be the highlight of four incredible and diverse weeks, a memory that is, however, happily etched in our minds forever!

Travel Agents, Tour Operators and Itineraries

Although you may think that the person you have on safari with you is your camp's 'client', you may be wrong. The international tour operator is the lifeline to most safari camps in Africa. More often than not, at least 50 per cent of bookings can come through a handful of tour operators; this figure can range to between 90 per cent and 100 per cent for some safari camps.

The guest you have in your camp is seldom your client. The tour operator or travel agent has chosen to send that person to your camp, over and above the many other camps in your region. The guest is the client or customer of the tour operator.

One particular tour operator may send one-tenth of the business your safari camp enjoys in a year. There are a number of instances where you as a guide can sour the relationship and flow of bookings from one or more agents. One agent who gets negative feedback from clients will often tell another agent. Bad news spreads far more quickly than good news! You can lose a lot of business by not understanding the relationship between the operator, the visitor and the safari camp for whom you work.

Very few guides realise the amount of hard work, time and effort that goes into getting one bum in a bed! Agents and operators spend vast sums of money on brochures each year, and can choose to put your camp into their attractive and alluring pages. Further costs go into advertising in various magazines, newspapers, and on radio and television.

Various journalists and travel agents are sent out at the international tour operator's expense. Long hours are spent at travel shows trying to influence the public to come to your country and safari camp. Slide and video evenings with drinks and snacks are laid on by the tour operator to hopefully plant a seed of interest and desire in a small percentage of the audience. Numerous phone calls on toll-free numbers (calls at the agents expense) may result in a booking, followed by masses of paper work, booking requests via fax or email, itineraries, invoices, confirmation vouchers, etc. Despite all the work, time and stress that goes into winning a booking, a high percentage can often result in a cancellation. When an agent does secure a booking, it is much valued and taken very seriously.

The owners of your safari camp may have spent years pursuing, nurturing and developing a strong relationship with various tour operators and agents.

A few hints follow on how to keep the tour operator who supplies your camp with guests happy:

- Give the guests value for money, and an unforgettable experience wherever possible. If you give them a mediocre time and they are treated professionally at the other camps they may visit after yours, this information will be relayed back to the agent who will then begin to doubt the standard and reliability of your camp. If they happen to get another poor report on your style and attitude to guiding, they may move their business to one of your competitors. They don't want unhappy clients requesting refunds. Your camp may then lose a potential 500 bed-nights from one operator alone.

- While casually discussing your guests' continued itinerary at the dining table or campfire, by all means offer some suggestions on how they can enjoy the areas and camps they are about to visit. You may know a guide at a particular camp who shares interests that are similar to theirs. Tell them about this guide and consider writing a letter of introduction.

- Never run down your guests' itinerary, even if you think the other camps they will be visiting are not good operations. Let them find this out by themselves. They can then raise the issue with their agent on their return. If you have planted a negative seed, they may mention this to the agent, saying you also advised them that a particular camp was not up to scratch. The last thing the person who supplies you with business wants is a guide trying to insinuate to the guest that the agent doesn't know his or her business!

- You may have developed a sound knowledge of the tourist industry in your country and in neighbouring countries. Help your guests plan their next safari holiday. You can recommend new areas, camps and guides. But be sure to tell your guest to book and discuss all that you suggest through the agent who sent them to you!

- The guests may be going on to Cape Town. You may know a restaurant with fine food and a lot of character, or a wine farm with good wines and great Cape Dutch architecture. They may be stopping over in London on the way home, so suggest your favourite pub. All this will show that you are not just there to show them wildlife, but that you are genuinely interested in helping them to enjoy their holiday as much as possible.

- **Never** influence your guests to book directly with your camp on their next visit; it will drive the agent absolutely berserk when they find out (and they will!). Word of your unethical behaviour will soon spread around the industry. If all the agents think you are going to try and turn the clients they spent so much time and money sourcing, they will treat you like the plague. The savings on tour operator commissions, by having one group of guests booking direct with you, are never worth the masses of business that you will lose from a constant supply of guests from that agent. You don't want to be classed as a tourist pimp, trying to solicit clients away from their agents. Stick to guiding and don't put your nose into areas that do not involve guiding and conservation.

'Don't bite the hand that feeds you'

Professional Whingers

These days there are a number of people who travel the world and seek any means to obtain a sizeable refund from their agent. They are professional whingers and they find fault in all sorts of ridiculous areas, making mountains out of molehills on their return. This type of person will often threaten to sue the agent. In order to keep a good name and avoid exorbitant lawyers' fees, the agent will often offer a large refund. Ensure that you are not roped in by this despicable type of person by any supportive comments you may have made while trying to please and befriend him or her on safari. Never badmouth your supplier to anyone at any time as they are often your biggest source of income.

This type of traveller can also threaten to put a 'hate page' on the World Wide Web which could include the name of your safari company. Let's say you work for 'African Safaris Unlimited' and you have a web page on the Internet, which prospective clients can look up. The professional whinger can create a page called the 'African Safari Unlimited Hate Page', which will come up next to your page on the web's directory. On this web page will be all the derogatory remarks from the guest about how terrible your safari camp is and all that went wrong. Hardly a good advert to have next to the web page that is meant to be promoting your operation. In return for the 'hate' page being removed, large sums of money may be requested. It is often paid to stop negative advertising.

'Dangerous game'

The Tides of Tourism

One of the exciting things about living in Africa is the unknown. It is a continent that is still guided by instinct and not quite by the requisites of the First World. Various African countries, acting on wild impulses, also have their downsides. One never knows when the big tourism wave your country has for so long enjoyed riding is going to break. Politics and politicians can set a thriving tourist industry back ten years by just one speech or military action. It does not matter how high the tourism standards are, or how good the guides are reputed to be, or how high the wildlife concentrations are. Tourists don't risk their lives, or spend their holiday dollars, in countries that are in the limelight of political violence, fuel shortages or general uncertainty.

For many years Kenya was the most sought-after tourist destination in Africa. Their parks gradually became overcrowded and had too many minibuses and safari vehicles vying for prime position at the various animal sightings. Political turmoil and violence created hot air thermals, which brought the media vultures tracking in from all directions. It wasn't long before the highlights of each incident, no matter how isolated, were being screened into every living room around the world.

Hot news and media competition ensure that TV stations are not only up to date, but exciting to watch. Who wants to spend a well-earned holiday in a political hotspot?

Zimbabwe's tourism went from full steam to bust in one heartbeat just before its elections in 2000. After the elections, continued political turmoil, fuel shortages and bad press resulted in a number of camps closing down, with guides leaving to work in neighbouring countries.

Never take your customers for granted; the steady stream of income from the tourism tap can be turned off in an instant.

'The tides of tourism'

Awareness

Being aware of all that goes on around you on safari is obviously imperative, but don't let it end there. Continue this sense into everything else that you do, be it around camp, at the airport, in town, etc. You never know who is around, listening and watching how you portray your true self.

> While waiting to meet up with a guide who was to take us on safari into the Okavango Delta, I was sitting across the road from Maun Airport at a small outdoor restaurant enjoying the sun and watching some of the characters that make up this colourful town. A vehicle drove up with the name of the safari company that was about to take us on our wildlife adventure into the depth of the delta. The guide climbed out and began speaking to some of his friends close to where I was sitting. They asked what he was up to. He told them he was about to embark on a safari with another boring bunch of tourists for a whole week!
>
> You can imagine what kind of impression I had of our new guide before the trip had even begun. Once we all met up inside the airport, he had on all his best tourist manners, a million-dollar plastic smile and standard clichés about how much he loved the bush, guiding and people!

Material Goods

When in the company of your clients, be it around a campfire, dining table, lounge or bar area, try not to discuss your material possessions. Your clients have placed you on a pedestal as someone totally dedicated to wildlife and nature, enjoying the simple things in life, unmaterialistic, uncluttered and unaffected by the assets that symbolise class, wealth and position. So if you happen to own the latest Mercedes Benz or an apartment in Knightsbridge, a houseboat on Lake Kariba, or a house in Cape Town, shares in the New York stock exchange, a bank account in Liechtenstein, don't talk about them. It will change their view of you, and they may begin to judge you by your assets.

If you are a director or shareholder of the safari company, try to keep this out of any discussion. I have listened to guides who have been given a title in a safari company and who have attempted to elevate their position to the clients by informing them of their various titles and position, trying to appear more than 'just a guide'. There is nothing wrong in being 'just a guide'. It is how you portray yourself to all around you, but especially to yourself that is important. Don't try to be something that you are not. Keep things simple; be focused and dedicated to your beliefs and wildlife. Your clients will appreciate you all the more for that.

If they perceive you are becoming high-powered, materialistic and wealthy, they will think you have lost your youthful innocence and love and understanding for all things wild. They rub shoulders each day with people trying to promote their egos through title and material image; it is a breath of fresh air for them to meet someone unaffected by these shallow and meaningless milestones in life. By all means buy what you desire, enjoy things to the full, but refrain from letting everyone know about it.

Stories

You may have a host of amazing wildlife stories from personal incidents and those of others in the wildlife industry. Don't retell them to guests if the stories are going to scare them about a certain animal or safari activity. These accounts may be humorous to you, but may affect the sleep of a nervous listener.

If some of your clients are about to go on a canoeing safari after leaving your camp, don't come out with all the hippo attack stories that you know. If they are about to begin a walking trail and there happened to be an incident in that area where a charging buffalo was shot the previous week, don't think you are gaining any status by telling them about this. It may ruin their whole walking experience by starting them off on a nervous and negative footing. Refrain from all the hyena and lion attack stories while around the campfire. These will play on the minds and sleep of many of the wide-eyed listeners. Don't portray the bush as a place of continual, potential danger; rather open their eyes and minds to its many joys and beauties.

Hunting Stories

As mentioned earlier, very few professional hunters fit comfortably into the guiding role, for no other reason than that they have worked in a different culture of the wildlife and tourism industry. During the hunting 'off season', a number of hunters pick up freelance work as guides with various lodges and safari camps. Normally this is to get them by in the lean months. Most do what is expected of them, but it is really a means to pass the time and earn a few extra dollars until the first hunt of the next season begins. If you are one of these hunter/guides, try and steer clear of hunting stories with standard tourists, bunny lovers, tree huggers, bleeding hearts (call them what you will) as they are not into blood-and-gore stories. Although there may be positive facts to back up hunting, don't throw them into a collection of people who have come out on a photographic safari and can't understand the reason behind a hunter pulling the trigger on a bush buck, giraffe, elephant etc., which only to be mounted among a collection of glass-eyed, lifeless mammals on a wall back home. There are a number of brilliant naturalists, conservationists and bushmen who have hunted for most of their working lives. If you are one of them and are standing in as a guide, try not to use past hunting experiences as a means to illustrate a point or pass on information about a certain animal. Keep the blood-and-gore out of the story. You will be proud of your profession, but there are people who can't and never will understand blood sports.

'Gore stories'

Camp Staff

It is never pleasant walking into a camp with a tense atmosphere among the staff. Camp life is often more difficult than living an urban lifestyle because you are around each other for sixteen hours each day and up to sixty days at a time. This lifestyle, combined with a continuous inflow of guests from all walks of life, each with a different set of needs and desires, plus all the various crises that safari life can come up with behind the scenes and at the most inopportune time, can wear down the most tolerant of people.

Treat your junior staff with respect and understanding. They also feel the stress of long days, isolation and a confined workplace. Be courteous, thoughtful, considerate, rational, understanding, honest, firm and fair. The genuine beaming faces that can often be found in a number of safari camps are not there just because of the size of the pay packet. The warmth and friendliness projected from your staff is often due to their pride, security and wellbeing in their workplace.

Your guests will pick up your rapport with the junior staff, your peers and superiors. The only way to gain the respect of all around you is to lead by example. Show that you are not scared to put in an honest, hard and long day's work on a continuous basis without letting any cracks show.

Make sure that your staff are well presented, clean, and clothed in the appropriate manner. Staff in tatty clothes, shoes and hats will be a reflection of your safari camp and its standards. Take an interest in how your staff look. If a shirt hangs out, request that it be tucked in. That person will realize that you have high standards and expectations.

National Parks and Neighbourly Relationships

Safari work is normally in wild and isolated areas, so you need to be on good terms with all your neighbours. It is often a small and intimate society; you all need one another at some time or other. You never know when your vehicle may break down, or when you may find yourself completely stuck in the mud or sand, need a spare part, ice, drinks, food, radio, etc. Don't destroy a good neighbourly relationship (often with your competition) by being over-zealous, competitive, surly and unfriendly. Most people in rural communities get on with each other very well and form close-knit relationships.

Form a good relationship with the national parks representatives in your area. Introduce yourself when the opportunity arises. Tell them who you are and for whom you work. Try to learn as much as you can from them, as they often have a wealth of knowledge about the area; some game scouts have been stationed in one park for over twenty years.

Everyone has something to teach you, you just need to know what it is and how to open it up without being offensive. Get to know the local research officer and find out what that person is studying. They are often shy, retiring intellectuals. If you show a genuine interest, you can learn a huge amount from them. Most park headquarters have good reference libraries and archives on past research in the park. Go through as much of this as you can. It will give you a sound understanding of the area.

Don't break park rules, which can result in fines and the souring of a good relationship that may have been built up by your colleagues and peers over the years. If you are not allowed to drive off the roads and there is a lion sighting some distance from the road, don't break rules to impress and attempt to gain favour with your clients at the expense of the good name of your company. Never offer a bribe to any parks, police or government official! You will begin to dig your own grave in that area and your future in the tourist industry will be short-lived. It's a no-win virus. If you can't obtain something through legitimate means, it is not worth risking all for which you have worked and strived. If you know of others that survive by these means, you can be assured that sooner or later things will become sour for them. Be proud of all that you achieve through honest procurement. You will be appreciative of it in the long run.

'As a guide, don't bribe'

Risks

By now it must be obvious that you must not take risks with your guests' lives or limbs; but don't forget their valuable camera equipment and binoculars. These days there is such a variety of gizmos and gadgets that clients bring on safari and all of it very expensive and the result of hard-earned cash. Don't take a foolish risk, which may jeopardise any of this equipment. Be especially careful when in the vicinity of water. If you have guests boarding a boat, canoe or mokoro, help them and their equipment in and out of the vessel. If driving the boat always bear in mind all the

155

water-sensitive equipment that you have on board.

The same applies to a canoe. You may think it fun to go through an obstacle course of fallen trees to show off your great canoeing and manoeuvring skills, till you hit a submerged stump and flip the canoe, not only stressing everyone out because of crocodiles, etc, but also resulting in the total loss of

'Don't gamble. Their lives and equipment don't belong to you.'

precious equipment which can't be replaced during the safari. Your camp may be the first safari destination of a month-long itinerary and now your guests will be without video, binoculars or camera. Not only will you be very unpopular, but you will have ruined their opportunity of recording their wildlife holiday. They may have spent years saving up to buy that particular set of equipment, so don't become blasé. Keep all this in mind.

Breaking the Rules

No matter how well you become accustomed to working amongst wildlife and what is rated as 'Dangerous Game' don't get to the stage where you become complacent and think you are 'Bullet Proof'. There are always animals and people out there to prove you wrong when you least expect it. When you let down your guard and don't follow the principles you have lived, worked and taught by, you will eventually pay a painful price.

I had just finished a busy and successful safari season and flown out my last safari guests who were well known personalities in the African wildlife industry. I was elated at finishing on such a high. I had flown to Botswana where I was traveling around by myself to a variety of premium safari camps. I was familiarizing myself with the various properties as I was about to embark on a trip around Australia to market a variety of lodges for a particular safari company.

I had been through a few of the camps where I was spoiled with an exclusive vehicle and guide. It was late September and animal populations and behaviours were at their peak, I had taken a multitude of amazing photographs and couldn't wait to show these gems to the Australian public and travel operators.

I had come to Savuti Camp which had a unique photographic 'hide' built of huge leadwood logs in an open square, only metres from one of the busiest waterholes in Africa. The boreholes which feed this pan couldn't keep up with the consumption by multitudes of animals who attempted to satisfy their thirst each day. Every night the elephant siphoned out the entire contents of the lodge's swimming pool.

In the afternoon while sitting in the hide alone, I was surrounded by over 100 elephant who had marched long distances to this isolated water hole. I sat in the safety of the hide, watching and photographing to the accompaniment of thirsty screams, rumbles and trumpets as they all jostled for an opportunity to drink from these life giving waters.

Early the following morning I went down alone to the hide. Within the confines of the 'Log Pile Hide' I wedged my camera between the gaps in the logs and photographed a never ending procession of zebra and wildebeest as they filed down to the pan. I couldn't get quite comfortable or in the right position to take what I thought would be the 'perfect shot'. I threw caution to the wind and took the canvas chair from within the hide and wedged it into some of the logs on the outside of the hide. My silhouette now covered by the logs behind me, I settled down to burn up numerous rolls of film as a stream of baboons, zebra, warthog, impala, kudu and wildebeest drank unsuspecting, only metres from me and my overworked camera.

My bearbanger was not on my belt where it lives for every safari day of the year, it was in my camera bag. I had no escape route from where I sat, but I fooled myself that elephant only came down to drink at lunch time and I would be out of there by then. All the rules I abide by when guiding guests began to fall by the wayside, and complacency at having no guests to look after began to set in. I was alone, euphoric and feeling more bullet proof by the minute.

I had ten minutes left in the hide before I had to go up to the camp and get ready for my flight to the next camp. It was the first lull in wildlife activity since I had been down there that morning. I was reading the learned words from Derek and Beverly Joubert's book; 'Hunting with the Moon' when unexpectedly four grey ghosts floated silently past me. I was elated, four elephant bulls, my favorite animal, rushed through what was left of the waterhole and desperately sucked from the fresh water pipe that slowly topped up the pan. 'What a great send off' I thought as my camera shutter rapidly snapped away.

Out the corner of my eye, which was pressed into the camera body I noticed more movement. A small family of elephant cows and calves hurried past me to drink, their bums only metres from here I sat. I now realised that I was in a tight spot and as soon as the first opportunity arose, would have to move quickly from where I was wedged into the front of the hide and climb into the safety of its confines.

Sadly that moment never came. Suddenly the area where I sat darkened as a huge cow with beautiful matching tusks, possibly the matriarch, halted on her way to the pan and stared down at me. I fell beneath her shadow and the piercing glare of a fiery orange eye that had seen other two-legged beasts shoot members of her family only eight years ago when hunting had stopped in this concession. She put her head down and charged, lifting my body onto one of the logs. I had both hands on her enormous forehead, only inches from my eyes. I recall seeing the small particles of mud imbedded between the little round grey dots that make up elephant skin. The short hairs on her forehead prickled the palms of my hands. Her pungent elephant smell filled my nostrils. She pinned me down, my hands feebly pushing against her giant head; I felt great pressure on my chest. I couldn't believe how my luck had changed! One minute I was sitting there reflecting on how fortunate I was and the next I was being squashed to death. This was my retribution for breaking the rules I had survived by all these years.

She stood back up, towering over my pitiable form, now lying prostate in an under veldt of elephant dung which covered the ground. I was trying to pull away from her; my right leg lay useless as it dragged by my side awkwardly. I pulled myself across the dirt on my hands like a paralyzed beggar. As she stood over me I looked around and assessed my situation; my favourite shirt was torn apart, my beloved camera lay open on the carpet of dung, my one shoe was off and the other broken. As she put her head down and came again, I saw my hat fly through the air and hit her on the wide part of her trunk. I had unknowingly thrown it at her; she stepped back and stood tall looking down at my pathetic form when suddenly I heard the familiar whoosh as a bear banger smoked past me and exploded above her. With this she turned and ran off. This was closely followed by a second banger and the whole herd stampeded off. I lay there feeling such a fool having caused so much disruption to these intelligent beasts who had walked so far to slake their thirst. The camp manager and his assistant had both fired the bear bangers that they were required by company policy to carry, thus extracting me from probable death.

I was flown out by helicopter to Maun and then by medical evacuation jet and rushed into one of South Africa's best trauma hospitals. There I spent the next four days in intensive care. I had sustained a dislocated femur, broken hip, fractured pelvis, broken ribs and fractured vertebrae.

I have recovered one hundred per cent and am extremely fortunate to have been spared by an animal that could have squashed the life out of me within seconds and by two guides who were living by the rules that they had been taught. I broke the laws that we live by in association with wild animals. I hope my lesson will save any other guides the trauma of being blinded by complacency.

Cleanliness and Hygiene

We have already discussed personal cleanliness. Ensure that this ethic carries through to the crockery and cutlery which your guests will use. The most common safari sickness is that of an upset stomach. This debilitating illness can put a client down for many hours or even days. Not only is it a waste of precious safari time, it is not pleasant feeling sick. If you are on an overland camping safari, walking, canoeing or extended rafting trip, ensure that all plates and glasses are thoroughly washed in boiling, soapy water at least once a day. Discard chipped and cracked plates, cups, saucers and glasses, as they do not present a good image.

If you are cutting the salad, laying out the food etc., ensure that the hands that were scratching around in some elephant dung an hour earlier have been washed and that the Swiss army knife being used to slice the tomatoes has also been cleaned.

Be extremely mindful of food that has been kept in a cooler box for an extended period. Don't ever use meals that have gone back into the fridge for the second or third time. Food poisoning is one of the most debilitating experiences that anyone could be unfortunate to contract in any situation, especially in an isolated and rustic situation. Be especially careful of chicken, fish and cold meats. If you are in any way uncertain as to its freshness, even if it smells OK, rather be on the safe side and throw it out.

- Ensure that all food has been thoroughly cooked.
- Try to serve it soon after preparation.
- If it must be reheated, do it thoroughly, almost re-cook it and do this once only!
- Don't mix raw and cooked food together.
- Make sure that everyone that assists in the preparing of a meal washes his or her hands thoroughly and repeatedly in hot water and Milton or a similar type of steriliser.

- Protect the food from insects, scavengers, pests and rodents.
- Water should be boiled or treated with chemicals to ensure it's not contaminated.

If you are leading an overland camping, walking, canoeing or rafting expedition, you are not only there to guide. Although you may have efficient and experienced staff, they are also human and can forget things or slip up in the most basic areas. Ensure that the tents are well-sited and clean, rubbish bins empty and that the loos have toilet paper. Make sure that the toilet facilities are well sited to ensure privacy, have a view where possible, and are clean. There should always be a basin of clean water, soap and a towel outside a bush loo. The same facilities must be provided before each and every meal.

Check the toilets again at dawn. Ensure that they are clean and presentable and that there is sufficient loo roll. Before the first guests come down for tea and coffee at the fire, make sure there are no empty beer or wine bottles, cigarette ends and bottle tops lying around, as these are not a pleasant sight on a pristine morning.

When out on safari activities always carry a loo roll and matches. When your guests need to make a 'pit stop', ensure they are well briefed on burning their loo roll. They shouldn't bury it beneath a stone or log as it may soon be exhumed by an inquisitive hyena, honey badger or baboon. Used loo roll is not a welcoming sight in a natural area, or any area. Make your guests well aware of fire hazards when burning their used loo roll. If you happen to be in an area of extensive dry grassland, rather supply a hand trowel to bury the used paper deep into the soil.

Safari camps often attract a number of snakes due to location, warmth, food, rats etc. A foolproof, snake catching tool is a two metre length of black PVC piping, 50mm wide and doubled over at one end and tied with wire. Approach the snake, pointing the open end of the pipe at the snakes head, the snake will usually take the opportunity to seek refuge in the dark hole. Once the snake is in the pipe, lift the pipe vertically. It is now safely captive and you are free to release it where you wish.

Routine

Every single job has a certain amount of routine! Don't think that because you are now in an exciting profession, every day will be like champagne corks blowing off. When you discover that guiding comes with a certain amount of routine, don't hold this against your employers or your chosen vocation. It occurs in every profession and is a normal part of everyday life. Learn to accept and understand this from your first working day.

Chapter 9

Medical Matters

*'More mistakes are made by those who do not care
than by those who do not know...'*

There's nothing quite so annoying and frustrating as becoming ill while on holiday. Although sickness is unpredictable, a number of precautions can be taken to avoid it. This becomes increasingly important when one is travelling in remote regions where the nearest medical facilities may be hundreds of kilometres away.

As a guide you will be expected to be knowledgeable about local health hazards, and you should be well trained in an advanced first aid course. If you are guiding clients among dangerous animals, you must have the equipment and knowledge to render comprehensive medical care should anything go amiss.

This chapter is not meant to advise you on how to take care of each medical problem you may encounter. It is a guideline on the minimal medical equipment you require when out on safari. It is presumed that you will have attended at least one advanced first aid course. One of the best investments you can make as a guide is to participate in at least one advanced medic's course every two years; once a year if possible.

You may be the most knowledgeable guide in the industry, and your personality may be equal to that of the Pied Piper. But if you don't have a comprehensive medic's pack available at all times and if you are not proficient in using its contents, you will not be able to save life or limb in the unplanned event of a serious injury to one of your clients.

'You're the Doc'

Danger!

There are a variety of different animals and elements that can cause injury, sickness or discomfort to your visitors. The sun is possibly the most dangerous of all. If guests don't respect the African sun and are not correctly informed as to its dangers, severe sunburn, heat fatigue and sunstroke may occur.

The dangerous animals which could possibly injure your guests are buffalo, elephant, lion, rhino, hippo, crocodile and hyena. Bees can be life-threatening if they attack in large numbers. Stinging ants, various wasps, spiders, scorpions and stinging nettles can make life quite uncomfortable. Snakebite is not common, but can cause a high degree of stress, pain and possible death if the patient isn't evacuated to competent care in time.

A number of other incidents may occur in safari life. Guides need to know how to administer first aid in the eventuality of drowning, electric shock, vehicle accidents, gunshot wounds, broken limbs, heart attack, asthma, epilepsy, childbirth, burns and scalding, blisters, boils, toothache, concussion, poisoning, convulsions, mountain sickness, dehydration, hysteria, drug overdose, hypothermia, diabetes, malaria and general sicknesses like diarrhoea, eye and ear infection, flu, migraine, etc.

It is beyond the scope of this book to be totally comprehensive, but the following few medical tips should be useful.

Perhaps the commonest, most inconvenient and debilitating sickness is traveller's diarrhoea. Here again, prevention is better than cure. The water source must be critically evaluated. If necessary, water should be boiled, filtered and treated before drinking. Even ice cubes made from tap water could be contaminated. Exercise caution with regard to any food that has been cooked, allowed to cool, and then re-heated. Do not mix raw and cooked food.

While on a canoe trip down the Zambezi with 16 Canadians, we ate with vigour and relish some precooked pizzas, covered with salami. That night, shortly after midnight, I was woken by the tent companions of four of the Canadians who had been hit by violent food poisoning, all within minutes of one another. One of the party had defecated in his bed. The others were vomiting and filling the chemical loos at an alarming rate. As I was trying to help these poor people, I suddenly became ill. We felt so sick, helpless, weak and dirty. The following day we worked out that the five of us had eaten from the pizza, which had salami on it which must have gone off. It was an unpleasant price to pay.

One cannot visit Africa without receiving a few insect bites or stings. The vast majority of these are unimportant but spider, scorpion and snakebite are among the most fear-engendering. The bites from some spiders and scorpions can result in serious poisoning, but their incidence is so rare that it is unnecessary to carry antivenom in the field. Supportive treatment will usually be all that is required. Although *snakebites* are more common, the value of carrying a snakebite kit in the bush is questionable. This is because snakebite antivenom is heat sensitive and must be carefully stored in a refrigerator. There is a very high incidence of severe life-threatening allergic reaction associated with the administration of antivenom. Consequently, it should only be administered by qualified medical personnel who have the facilities available for intubation and respiratory support. Any victim of snakebite therefore should receive intensive resuscitation and supportive treatment, and should be evacuated immediately to a hospital.

Prevention is better than treatment. Common sense dictates that one must:
• Wear closed shoes in the bush.
• Look where one is walking.
• Wear shoes at night, particularly around a campfire.
• Zip up the tent and tuck in one's mosquito net.
• Never try to handle snakes, as some are excellent at feigning death
  – e.g., rinkhals and Mozambique spitting cobra.

Remember, snakes are always more frightened of humans than vice versa.

The following are the *suggested medical requirements* that should be available while guiding in a remote area. It is wise to have a central area, i.e. the base camp where most of the medical equipment is kept, and smaller medic kits in the vehicles, boats or canoes. When out walking one should have a basic resuscitation kit available. You can never have enough triangular bandages and field dressings.

The main medical kit in camp should be kept in a cool and accessible place, checked regularly and restocked. The medications must be kept up to date. Should you be uncertain as to how to use the medications, it is absolutely imperative that you seek advice from suitably qualified personnel. With the advent of modern communications (satellite phones, HF radios etc.), advice should be available easily and at any time.

These lists are in no way meant to provide for every medical malady that can occur, but with this equipment you should be able to provide a comprehensive first aid service to your clients or camp staff.

Medic's Pannier - Base Camp

1. Resuscitation		Quantity
Heavy duty scissors		1
Oro-pharyngeal airways, sizes 3 & 4		2
Ambu bag		1
Neck brace e.g: collar foam		1
Arm sling e.g: collar foam 2 m		1 roll
Field dressings 15 x 15 cms		5
Gauze swabs 75 x 75 mm (100)		2 packs
Cotton wool bandage 100 mm (Velband)		5
Cotton bandages (Kling)	50 mm	5
	100 mm	5
	150 mm	5
Cotton crepe bandages (Elastocrepe)	50 mm	5
	100 mm	5
	150 mm	5
Adhesive tape (Elastoplast)	50 mm	2
'Micropore' plaster	25 mm	2
Strip plasters (Band Aid) box of 25		2

2. IVI Kit		
Vacolitres - Ringer's Lactate 1 litre		3
- Normal saline 1 litre		3
- Rehydration fluid 1 litre		3
- ½ strength Darrows/Dextrose x 200mls		3
IVI Admin. set		3
Cannulas 18 + 20 - assortment		6
Adhesive strips - (Opsite)		5
Adhesive tape - (Zinc oxide) 25 mm		2

3. Suture Kit	
Instruments	
Needle holder	1
Fine artery forceps	2
Non-toothed tweezers	1
Scissors	1

Suture material, assorted sizes 3/0, 4/0
  Nylon   5
  Chromic catgut   5
Skin stapler kit   1
Local Anaesthetic kit - Dental syringe   1
  - 27 guage dental needles   20
  - Lignocaine cartridges 2 mls   20
  - Lignocaine ampule 20 mls x 1%   2

4. Injectable Medication

Adrenaline 1:1000 1 cc   3
Antihistamine - Promethazine HCl 50mg/2mls
  e.g: Phenergan   3
Anti-inflammatory - Diclofenac 75 mg/3mls
  e.g: Voltaren   5
Antispasmotic - Hyoscine 20mg/ml
  e.g: Buscopan   3
Anti nausea - Prochlorperazine mesylate 12.5 mg/ml
  e.g: Stemetil   3
Cortisone - Hydrocortisone 100 mg/ml
  e.g: Solu Cortef   3
Syringes 5 cc   10
Needles 18 + 20   10 of each
Alcohol prep. swab - e.g: Webco   20

5. Oral Medication

Put into zip lock bags with clear labels and dosing instructions. A list should be included which details the medication to be used for each malady.

Aspirin - Acetylsalicyclic acid   e.g: Disprin   20
Paracetamol - Acetaminophen   e.g: Panado   20
Paracetamol/Codeine   e.g: Panacod   20
Ibuprofen   e.g: Brufen   20
Loperamide   e.g: Imodium   20
Prochlorperazine mesylate 5mg   e.g: Stemetil   20
Hyoscine butylbromide 10mg   e.g: Buscopan   20
Amoxycillin   e.g: Amoxil   2 x 15
Co-trimoxazole   e.g: Bactrim   2 x 20

Ciprofloxacin	e.g: Ciprobay	2 x 10
Doxycycline		2 x 10
Quinine sulphate		2 x 10
Loratadine	e.g: Clarityne	2 x 10
Celestamine		2 x 10
Prednisone 5mg		2 x 10
Zopiclone	e.g: Imovane	1 x 10
Valium 5mg	e.g: Pax 1 x 10	
Valoron drops 10mls VERY POTENT PAIN KILLER		
REQUIRES PRESCRIPTION		1

6. Ointments

Paraffin in gauze/Tullegra strips	10 x 2
Antiseptic cream e.g: Betadine ointment 30g	2
Savlon ointment 30g	2
Hydrocortisone cream 20g	1
Antihistamine e.g: Anthisan 20g	1

7. Miscellaneous

Electrolyte rehydration powder - Darrow-Liq	10 packets
Eyepads	5
Asthma pump - Ventolin inhaler	1
Cold remedies e.g: Flustat	1
Oil of cloves - toothache	
Eye: Local anaesthetic drops: MIMS anaesthetic and MIMS fluorescent stain	5
Antibiotic eye ointment e.g: Occ. Chloro 1% eye ointment	2
Micropore plaster 5mm	1
Malaria test kit	5
Sterile gloves size 7 ½	4 pairs
Unsterile gloves large	10 pairs
Savlon/Hibitane sachets 20mls	10
Eardrops e.g: Sofredex	1
Thermometer	3
Stethoscope	1
Safety pins	20

Oxygen is an invaluable addition in most stressful and debilitating situations. These days oxygen field sets are readily available from most First Aid outlets.

Medical Pack for Vehicle, Boat and Canoe

The minimum suggested contents are listed below and should be immediately available. The pack should be totally waterproof in the event of rain or if the boat, canoe or mokoro capsizes.

Airway	1 set
Triangular bandages	3
Field dressings	2
Scissors	1 pair
Crepe bandages 50mm	1
150 mm	2
Sterile gloves size 7 ½	2 pairs
Elastoplast 50mm	2
Vacolitre Ringer's lactate	2
Cannula	2
Admin. set	2

Tablets

Painkillers - Paracetamol e.g: Panado	10 of each
Anti nausea - Prochlorperazine mesylate 5ml e.g: Stemetil	10
Anti diarrhoea - Imodium	10
Anti inflammatory - Ibuprofen e.g: Brufen	10
Anti allergy - Celestamine	10
Electrolyte rehydration powder - Darrow Liq	5 pkts

Injectables

Adrenaline	2
Antihistamine	2
Cortisone	2
Appropriate syringes and needles	
Webco swabs	
Asthma pump	1

Medical Pack for Walking

Contents should be similar to the Canoe pack but with smaller quantities in order to fit into a small daypack.

These are considered the minimum requirements for walking.

See under Medic's pannier - Base camp for details of drugs.

Field dressings	2
Triangular bandages	2
Scissors	1 pair
Sterile gloves size 7 ½	1 pair
Crepe bandage 50 mm	1
150mm	2
Injectables	
Adrenaline ampule	1
Antihistamine ampule	1
Cortisone ampule	1
Needles, syringes, Webco swabs	
Tablets	
Paracetamol	
Stemetil	
Imodium	
Ibuprofen - Brufen	
Airway	
Asthma pump	
Esmark rubber bandage for tourniquet	
Water purification tablets	
Vacolitre Ringer's lactate	1
Cannula	1
Admin. set	1

Client First Aid Kit

Clients should be advised to have a simple and basic First Aid kit with them. The contents should include:

Malaria prophylaxis tablets
Insect repellent - spray and roll-on
Imodium for gastro-enteritis
Stemetil for nausea
Simple Analgesics - Paracetamol
Sunblock lotion
Dark glasses
Their own current medication and oral contraceptives
One course of antibiotics
Antiseptic cream
Antihistamine cream
Micropore plaster
Band Aid strips

It will help you when guiding to know the medical history of your clients. Before each safari activity, ask if anyone is allergic, especially to bees, and whether antone is an asthmatic or has a medical condition about which you should know.

Indemnity Forms

The insurance companies that cover most safari camps for 'personal liability' normally require all guests to sign an indemnity form on their arrival. If your camp or safari operation has this requirement and the onus is on you to effect this formality, ensure that you do so. Although these indemnities often don't stand up in court, it is one less opportunity for the insurance companies to worm their way out of covering a claim.

If you have a guest who refuses to sign the indemnity form, ensure that you give your full safety briefing, and as comprehensively as you have ever done it, in front of all the other guests. This will ensure that you have other witnesses to your full and comprehensive briefing should a problem ever arise.

Malaria

As a guide working in a malaria area, ensure that you religiously take your malaria prophylactics. Should you not follow your course of medication, there is a strong chance that you will contract this debilitating illness. You will be of little use in your role as a guide. Your company may incur major expenses in evacuating you to the nearest doctor, clinic or hospital. The biggest danger is that malaria is life-threatening! It can kill and does so on a regular basis. Don't play roulette with Africa's most dangerous animal: Mrs Anopheles Mosquito. She kills more than a million people *each* year. It is quite easy to become her victim and it is equally simple to deny her the opportunity of wreaking havoc on your body!

During the malaria months, not only should you be taking a prophylactic, you must avoid being bitten. Use a mosquito net above your bed, ensure it has no holes or any opening for a mosquito to come in. In the evenings wear long sleeves and trousers. Put mosquito repellent on yourself. Make sure your camp is sprayed on a regular basis with a pyrethrin-based spray. When spraying the camp, don't forget to focus on all the staff quarters. Spray both inside and outside the rooms, under the thatch and in all the nooks and crannies where mosquitoes hide.

Every safari operation should ensure that all staff are supplied with adequate medication to prevent them from coming down with malaria. In addition, each camp should keep malaria tests in their fridges. Staff are vulnerable to malaria. If it is diagnosed early, there is time to treat it, which saves suffering and possibly death.

- Remember the Cs! Common sense and a confident calmness, coupled with good communication.
- With modern communication facilities, e.g., satellite phones, radios etc., medical advice is readily available.
- A guide who is well prepared will be able to handle most medical emergencies.

'Killer no. one'

Chapter 10

Photography and Equipment

'Some people have eyes for looking, but not for seeing'

Gone are the days when tourists came on safari with box brownies and cine-cameras. These days you seldom see a camera that does not have a self-wind film mechanism and automatic ASA settings. It's incredible to see the advancements that are being made in the photographic world of today. This area of the hi tech industry is forging ahead in leaps and bounds.

Digital is now the rage. It is amazing to watch guests download the scenes of their morning's game drive onto a powerful lap top computer, while seated at the breakfast table overlooking a waterhole, at a safari camp deep in the wilderness of Africa. Bemused camp staff and guests gather around the screen in awe and relive the settings and animals that were captured on a digital chip only minutes ago. The frames that don't fit into the 'accepted' category are deleted to the recycle bin. Should a phone link be close at hand, friends and family on the opposite side of the world can appreciate the highlights of the game drive at their breakfast table that same day!

Today's modern safari tourist comes armed with a small digital point-and-press camera, plus a digital video camera that can also double as a still camera. Such cameras can take flash photos at night and come equipped with infrared facilities. It is not uncommon to see a guest scuffle around in a large camera case while out on a night drive, only to produce a set of infrared, night binoculars, showing all before them as clear as day, but in a green hue.

Large quantities of very expensive equipment are brought out on safari by a growing number of visitors these days. As a safari guide, you need to be aware of the reason they have invested so heavily in all this equipment. And don't forget, they have lugged it all halfway around the world! This valuable equipment is seldom bought for show. Its owners, your clients, hope to put it to good use and to go home with some rewarding results. That is where you come in.

Photographic Knowledge

It is not possible, in the confines of a chapter, to outline everything you should know about photography. Volumes of books have been published on this subject. The object of this chapter is to give you an understanding of how to enable your clients to take photographs that will turn out to be unusual, exciting and memorable recordings of their safari.

As a guide you need to have a thorough understanding of photography.

Most of your clients will have a camera for recording their safari holiday. People enjoy taking photographs for a number of reasons.

- For sheer enjoyment. It's a hobby that gives them stimulating pleasure from the time they pack all their equipment before an expedition, to editing, filing, mounting and enlarging their results.
- To show friends and family back home what a great holiday their money gave them.
- To capture the perfect picture.
- As a memory of a once-in-a-lifetime holiday.
- As a commercial venture to sell, publish or make documentaries.

'You need to know'

No matter what the reason, you are the one who will be in a position to ensure either rewarding or mediocre results.

There is no better way to learn about photography than to take photos yourself.

Beware: a word of caution. This is an addictive hobby. There is very little to beat the joy of downloading your digital chip of photos and realizing that you have one or two mind-blowing photos. Large amount of adrenaline and bytes are burnt up when an animal scene becomes exciting, and your index finger fires away to the addictive sound of your shutter and the shutters around you!

Lifelong relationships between guide and client are formed with faces pressed into the back of cameras, noses pushed into most unsightly positions, twitching index fingers, and ecstatic noises emitted after a volley of shutter fire. Hours are spent in uncomfortable positions, often in silence, in quest of the perfect shot. Good-humoured banter is swopped about different makes of camera, chips and lenses.

Photography can be a love-hate pastime. It is an expensive hobby, but most guides don't have the overheads of rent, food, drinks, entertainment, transport, etc. It is through trial and error that you will learn about lighting, framing, anticipating and positioning. Armed with this knowledge you should be able to guide your clients towards getting good photographic results.

Most guides begin their photographic careers with an old hand-me-down camera and normally take prints, later changing to slides or video. These days guides have the opportunity to go straight into the incredible world of digital photography, saving so much money in development and film costs along with the opportunity to learn by taking multitudes of pictures that can be deleted and cost them nothing. Even a bad picture these days can be transformed into something quite acceptable with the use of that other great photographic tool 'Photoshop' as long as the picture isn't blurred.

Equipment

There is very little difference in the makes of cameras these days. You can own the best and most expensive camera equipment, but if you don't have an eye for a good picture and don't know how to use your equipment, the person with an old SLR camera, with screw-on lenses, manual rewind and a hand held, light metre, will end up with better results than yours.

As a young guide you probably will not be able to afford a modern and expensive camera and lenses. No problem; some of the best photos that I have ever taken were with a very old Russian Praktika, given to me by my parents for my 21st birthday.

Being in the ***right place*** at the right time helps a great deal. In your line of work you have the opportunity to be in the right place for 11 months of the year, each and every year, capturing all the colours and events of the ever-changing seasons.

The basic camera equipment you should acquire is:
- A SLR (single lens reflex) digital camera.
- A telephoto lens, 300 mm zoom if possible.
- A good, sturdy monopod.
- A wide angle zoom lens of between 24 mm and 75 mm, or whatever you can afford. The wider the lens the more expensive they become. There are a number of good pirate lenses that are not quite as expensive as the lenses that are the same make as your camera.
- UV and polarising filters, which will also prevent your lenses from being scratched.
- A jeweller's screwdriver set for emergency camera maintenance and repair work.
- A large 'puffer' for blowing out dust from cameras and lenses.
- Lens tissue and cleaning fluid.

Ensure that everything you buy is in good working order. Check the lenses for scratches and internal mould from moisture.

At a later date you may wish to acquire the following:
- Camera flash.
- A large telephoto lens.
- Tripod.
- Second camera body, compatible with all your lenses.
- Macro lens for flowers and insects.
- A waterproof 'Pelican' case for taking good care of your camera equipment.
- Slide projector.
- Slide screen.
- Slide box to arrange and prepare slide presentations.

If you have to make a choice between investing in a great camera body or the best camera lens, rather spend more on the lens. It is the glass through which you are shooting that is important. A better lens is generally a faster lens, with a wider aperture to allow you to photograph more low-light situations. Choose a lens with an "f" stop as close to 2.8 as your budget will allow.

The list of extra accessories can become endless. If, however you have most of the above equipment, you will be in a position to be as good as the best. This is quite possible because of your proximity to and understanding of wildlife.

Film

The choice of film is considerable. First you need to determine if you are going to use prints or slide film. The next choice is brand name, and then the speed of the film.

Prints

Most serious wildlife photographers do not use print film, as one can always make a print from a slide for a photo album or make a blow-up to be framed and hung on a wall. The one advantage of print film is that you can get a better quality, high speed (and by definition high grain) film in print format. This means you can photograph low-light scenes more easily and successfully with prints. You can buy print film with an ASA reading of 200 or 400 and get quite good photographs which show little grain in your result from low light situations. The same ASA rating for slide film is usually too grainy for any serious use, especially if you want to sell some of your slides, or produce a book at some stage in your life.

Slide Film

Most professional photographers and anyone who wants to sell photographs use slide film. Slides can be screened and shown to small and large audiences; or used in brochures, adverts, books, etc. These days it does not cost much to make prints from slides.

When shooting slide film don't go for high ASA films. The only time this high ASA will be appropriate is when there is very little light and you are witnessing a phenomenal scene. Always keep a box or two of fast film handy for such an event.

ASA refers to the 'speed' of the film and is marked clearly on the box and on the film itself. The higher the ASA rating or number, the 'faster' the film, i.e., you can photograph more easily in low-light situations. The more you increase the ASA rating, the more light the film will absorb. This in turn allows you to shoot at faster shutter speeds, resulting in less blurred images. However, the downside of this is that the faster films will show more grain on the photograph and less clarity and colour. For this reason most professional photographers will seldom use slide film at more than 100ASA.

Fuji 100 ASA slide is a good quality film that has the best colours for outdoor shots. There are two types of Fuji 100. The best is Fuji 100F - but it is the most expensive too. If you are on a budget, then go for Fuji 100 Sensia.

Spare Film

Living in an isolated situation makes film a precious commodity for guides. If a client runs out of film and you happen to have a spare roll with you, offer the roll to help out. This kind gesture will usually be highly appreciated by most guests and is often remembered for years to come.

Positioning and Framing

At the crux of all good photography is the appropriate positioning and framing of the subject.

Positioning involves the desired lighting and correct angle of the animal, tree, waterfall, flower, bird, person, etc. This is not always possible when working with unprogrammed wildlife, but it is important to keep this in mind as you approach your subject. Explain to your clients what you intend to do. Let them know that you understand their keen desire to capture this rare moment on celluloid, but explain the difficulties and risks of the animal running off or bird flying away.

If you are in doubt about where to park your vehicle, the golden rule is to try and park with the sun behind you, so that the light falls onto your subject and the camera can pick up its colours and tints. Sometimes a guest may want to photograph a backlit or silhouette of the subject against the sun. This can produce eye-catching and unusual results, but the average photographer will not be too comfortable with the compensated camera settings needed for an acceptable result.

Plan your game drive routes, if possible, so that your guests will not have to stare directly into the sun on a game drive. This will usually mean that in the morning you go out to the west and in the evening you travel towards the east. When you come back, guests won't have to stare into the late setting sun. This is only a guideline; obviously you should go where your gut tells you the greatest wildlife experience might be.

Keep your eye on the *sky*; watch the movement and direction of the clouds in relation to the sun. Always be aware of shadows; yours, the vehicle and one that may be cast by a tree or cloud. The shadow of your vehicle and its occupants may spoil the perfect picture of a leopard walking in rich morning light. Or it may make the picture by showing how close you were to this shy and secretive cat.

Be mindful of *wind* direction. If your much-feared human scents blow in the direction of a nervous breeding herd of elephant, you may only be able to photograph their shuffling hindquarters, framed by a cloud of dust.

Keep all human *noise* to a minimum. You may have spent a great deal of time and patience approaching your subject. A raised voice or metallic knock in a vehicle or boat could ruin all your hard work in an instant. Before quietly sneaking up to your subject, ask your guests to keep their voices down, and ensure there are no loose binoculars or lenses on a seat that could fall onto the floor and cause a noise that will frighten off the animal.

When in a vehicle or boat, switch your engine off once you are in position. Those guests with video cameras don't want the alien sound of an engine as background noise to their footage. It is impossible to take a photograph with a telephoto lens while an engine is idling. Remember that the noise emitted from an engine is unnatural, foreign and intrusive to a wilderness experience. Your guests would rather listen to the multitude of sounds that Africa has to offer, than to the noisy throb of a diesel or two-stroke engine.

Unnecessary *movement* can also put your subject to flight. There is no point in getting upset with your clients if they end up frightening off a carefully approached animal if you failed beforehand to ask them to keep still. Ask your guests to be mindful of movement too, when others are about to take a photo, as this can often cause blurring, especially when large telephoto lenses are being used.

Knowing the various habits of wild animals helps tremendously. Often you will be able to predict an animal's next move, direction or behaviour. With this intuitive knowledge you will be able to place your clients in the prime photographic position for the next scene in a wildlife drama.

If you are about to witness an amazing spectacle and some of your guests are keen on photography, mention the importance of having a good number of frames left on the roll in the camera. They wouldn't want to be changing film half way

'Positioning'

through the event. If a roll of film is nearly finished, encourage them to rewind and rather forfeit the few frames still left. By doing so they will be prepared with a new full roll, ready and loaded, to capture the unfolding spectacle.

Always ensure that you place your vehicle, boat and clients in a position for *them* and not *you* to get the best photographs! Don't loose sight of whose safari holiday it is.

Who is paying for the experience and who is being paid to provide that service?

As much as I would like to, I personally don't carry a camera at my side when conducting *walking safaris* in areas of dangerous game. I have missed capturing on film countless once-in-a-lifetime opportunities because of this. I have had to be satisfied with my photographs taken by my 'head camera'. Fortunately, this camera also records smells, sounds, sun and wind.

While walking a group of guests up to a potentially dangerous animal, you will already have a slightly cumbersome backpack, binoculars and rifle, and you don't need a camera flopping around your neck or at your side if the situation requires you to be nimble and manoeuvrable. The last thing your clients need when up close to a breeding herd of elephant, pride of lion or old male buffalo, is for you to be clicking away with your camera. Your main responsibility is to ensure their safety and enjoyment.

'Prepare for the right shot'

By all means keep your camera and appropriate lenses in your backpack. Should you encounter one of nature's many surprise incidents, but without a potentially dangerous animal in the immediate vicinity, use your camera if it is not going to offend your guests. If you are keen on photographing butterflies but your guests only want to see big game, it is not the appropriate time to be chasing an allusive insect around, pursuing your personal interest.

If you own a video camera, use it wisely on a vehicle or boat safari. I have witnessed guides telling their guests to shush so they can video their pet subject. Guides are reluctant to talk when taking their own video footage, and this means holding back knowledge they could be imparting to their **paying guests**.

Framing a situation is of critical importance if you want your guests to obtain optimum photographic results. This is something you have to train yourself to do, as the human eye sees in three dimensions, whereas a camera only 'sees' in two dimensions. When looking through the viewfinder, a tree in the background may seem far away, but the developed picture may show it growing out of the animal's back. You need to continually think about framing the subject.

Most of your guests will not be very experienced photographers. They would appreciate your hints and tips, which will teach them more about photography and help them to achieve better results. Try to help and advise your guests in a manner that will not make them feel foolish in front of others. Assess the situation when offering advice, as some people may not like being told what to do.

Be aware of trees, and try and use them as 'bookends' to frame a subject or setting rather than having them grow out of an animal's head. When photographing various animals (a herd of elephant, for example) advise your photographers to capture the scene when these large grey animals are slightly apart.

'Wise framing'

179

Then they wont be growing out of each other; or result in one elephant with six legs or two heads. Again, the processed film will give one a flat picture, without the picture-depth that one saw through the viewfinder.

Always be aware of the background. It is easy to become so focused on the subject that you forget to see beyond that. Look out for other vehicles that may be on the opposite side of the lion kill where you have positioned your own vehicle. There could be a road, building, water pump, windmill, power line, telephone line, a person or a safari camp in the background. Having any of these in the frame may spoil the essence of a picture.

If you do not have a practised photographic eye, or you don't have a camera and you want to get a feel for what a photograph will look like, take your fingers and make a small rectangle out of your thumbs and index fingers. The rectangle should be a maximum of one inch across. Hold this rectangle against your eye and you will get an idea as to what the photo will look like through a camera.

From the feet up is good advice to pass on to your clients, especially these days with auto-focus cameras. Most people point the camera at the centre of an animal. The camera focuses and they take the picture. It comes out minus any feet. They haven't let their eyeball swoop the whole way around the eyepiece to take in all that is or isn't in the frame.

When photographing an individual animal it is often advisable to have a narrow depth of field to isolate the subject. i.e., f.2.8 to f.4.6. If you are photographing a herd of animals, go to the extreme and set your camera at f.11 or higher and most the herd will be in focus. If using a heavy or powerful lens a monopod will ensure a better result.

If it is safe and you think your clients will get better photographic results, get them out onto the ground and on their bellies, up a tree, or on top of your vehicle. Once again, show enthusiasm and desire to obtain for them the best possible results under the circumstances. A keen photographer will not mind discomfort if there is a chance of capturing that ultimate photo for which that they are always searching.

I have enjoyed watching guests cover themselves with water hyacinth weed, slowly slithering through smelly mud, with only the whites of their eyes and teeth showing. All this in quest of the perfect picture.

Remember the 5 E's :

'Extra effort equals ecstatic enjoyment'

Experienced Eye

As a result of months and years of guiding, your eye will become tuned to settings, scenes and light, which could result in a memorable picture. Your clients will appreciate you pointing out a massive anvil of colourful cloud, blushed pink by a setting sun, framed by a dead tree in the foreground or a fish eagle perched on a dry limb, with two-thirds of old moon crowning its noble head or a range of mountains, clean and clear from recent rains, reflected in a glass-like river, flowing at their base.

You will know the behaviour an elephant displays just before swinging himself up onto his hind legs to stretch high into the tasty canopy of acacia leaves. Get your guests ready to capture this rare sight. When a courting lion rises from his slumber and begins to sniff his feline mate, prepare your guests to photograph the powerful mating display of this royal couple.

'Some people have eyes for looking, but not for seeing.
Open their eyes so they too can see.'

You are in a fortunate position to have an eye that has an understanding and appreciation for all that it has been privileged to see in its short life. An eye so fortunate that it is not having to look at a computer screen all day, four sterile white office walls, sheets of paper covered by letters and numbers, flickering fluorescent lights, nor have ears hearing the hum of the central heating, 68 floors above the ground! Make the most of this opportunity.

Gung Ho Attitude

This may be the first time that your guests have seen the animal or spectacle you are about to approach and photograph. Therefore, for the first photograph it is not necessary to get right up close. Take time and 'stalk' your subject, photographing as you get closer and closer. The first sighting of the animal or bird may be from fifty metres away; you may know that you can get to within twenty metres with reasonable certainty.

Rather stop at fifty metres and switch off the engine to photograph the subject from a distance. Your guests will have then 'bagged' their subject. If your subject moves away during your approach your guest won't feel too let down.

A photographer would rather waste a few frames and get a photo of the subject at fifty metres, then slowly move up, taking more photos at thirty five metres and then at twenty metres, rather than risk getting their first and only (albeit perfect) photo at twenty metres. If you were to move straight to the twenty metre mark, the photographer might not get any photos at all should the subject take off! Try calming down your guest, who may be an enthusiastic wildlife photographer, who has just missed his or her ultimate photograph, because the subject was chased away during a gung-ho approach!

'Stalk it don't balk it'

Digital Photography

Digital technology advances by the day. This exciting new form of photography is taking the world by storm. I am certain that digital photography will in time replace traditional photographic techniques. No more endless rolls of film, developing costs, slide mounting or frustration from 'binning' thousands of mediocre and unwanted images! Will terms like emulsions, f-stops, exposure and ASA settings give way to tech talk like Memory, CF Cards, bit depth, computer chips, LCD's and pixels?

As a guide you will be facing these new pieces of equipment on a daily basis. It is therefore good to have a basic idea of how digital photography works. The cameras come in all shapes and sizes and range in price from US\$300 to over US\$50,000. There are models to suit all users. Most digital cameras are similar to traditional point & shoot cameras but lately there are more and more digital SLR (Single Lens Reflex) cameras. The bodies of these cameras look the same as non digital SLRs, and their interchangeable lenses are their biggest advantage.

All cameras will record a picture by transmitting the light passing through the lens onto a light receptive medium. Conventional photography uses a 'wet' film base, a plastic base covered with chemicals, which reacts to the light in order to record the image. In a digital camera (or scanner) the film is replaced by a small computer chip called a CCD. This stands for a Charge Coupled Device. This chip converts light into a digital signal. Its surface is divided into tiny squares called pixels, each one recording a small segment of the image. Naturally, the more pixels available, the higher the resolution, sharpness and clarity of the image. A 'point and shoot' digital camera, at 640 x 480 pixels, would record sufficient resolution for holiday snaps and web page graphics, but images requiring publication in magazines require at least 1600 x 1200 pixels, or more.

Once the image has been exposed to the CCD, it has to be stored. The image is stored on memory cards, which are inserted into the camera much like a conventional camera film. Today there are different standards, Smartmedia, SecureDigital (SD) and Compactflash (CF). It seems that CF is the dominant standard at present, as it also supports tiny hard drives with big capacities like the IBM 1 GB Microdrive. Naturally, the higher the resolution, the larger the size of the digital file required for the recording of the image. Once saved onto the memory card, the image can then be downloaded to the hard drive of a computer. The easiest way to do that is on a laptop with a PCMCIA (or PC Card) slot. All the Memory cards can be inserted via an adapter in these slots and will be treated by the PC as a regular drive. The memory card of the camera can then be re-used. This digital format enormously reduces the running costs of photography. Another huge advantage of digital photography is that by using the LCD - this is the display panel on the back of the camera - one is able to see the recorded image immediately so all 'dud' photographs can be instantly 'culled'. This frees the memory of the camera, allowing more space for future images.

Just as conventional equipment requires a slide projector and a screen, so the digital camera requires a personal computer and printer with the appropriate software. The initial expenditure in digital equipment can be considerable, but once the equipment has been acquired one does not need to buy film or pay for processing.

Another huge advantage of digital photography is that you have in your home computer, screen and ink jet printer, a dark room virtually at your fingertips and can thus become very creative. All the standard darkroom operations can be performed without the wasted materials and chemical odours, etc.

The digital photographer can now easily do things that are traditionally extremely difficult or impossible. A lion's yellow eyes can be turned red for example, or a vehicle can be removed from the scene of a lion kill in order to create the perfect architectural photograph. It is possible to send these images by e-mail to all parts of the world, as well as to print them via your printer. Publishing images on the world wide web is thus very simple. Slide shows can be stored 'canned' – i.e: they can be stored on discs and instantly recalled for presentations without the hours of sorting required when searching for images in the celluloid format.

One other huge advantage of digital photography is that you immediately know what you have. Sometimes it takes a bit of tweaking to get the right exposure, angle or framing. With digital you can shoot until it is the way you want it to be, if, of course, the animal cooperates.

At present a number of professional wildlife photographers are moving from 'wet' film to serious exploration of the digital route, with highly satisfactory results.

The technique of the guide, in helping his clients to be in the right position at the right time, is the same.

In discussing digital photography, this quote may be relevant!

"It is not the strongest of the species that survives, nor the most intelligent, but the one most responsive to change." Charles Darwin.

Video

Only 20 years ago this amazing new introduction to photography was a camera body as long as your forearm, which passed a moving picture down a long umbilical cord to a heavy recorder, which hung from a shoulder. Today, nearly everyone on safari has one, but the battery is the size of a matchbox and can last up to three hours, the tape is not much bigger, and the whole unit fits into the palm of a human hand. It has a colour screen, records digitally and can take still pictures as well.

The beauty of video is that it can record sound and movement, quite a plus when around wildlife. It enables one to record the sound and movement of an elephant scooping sloppy mud into the crook of its trunk and then deftly throwing it onto any desired area of its large grey frame, while capturing the background song of an ever-alert drongo perched only metres above in a battered acacia tree. Video costs nothing to develop; its pictures can be played back on the camp TV or laptop that same day. Back at home, it can be edited down to a condensed memory of one's highlights.

Apart from positioning and framing, there is one new rule of which to be aware, and that is sound. Try to keep human and engine noise to a minimum. If there is only one person with a video and you know that the rest of the group would be interested in learning about the subject you happen to be watching, either speak in hushed tones or at opportune times.

Advice and Suggestions

Most of your guests will not be experienced photographers. If you can offer some friendly advice that will not embarrass them or spoil their fun, do so.

- Before each safari activity, encourage your guests to bring double the amount of film they think they need. Make sure they always have a spare battery.
- Keep all film out of the sun and heat.
- There are very fine greases in optical equipment. Therefore, never let cameras, lenses and binoculars lie in the sun.

'Always be on a roll'

- When in a vehicle, ensure that cameras and binoculars are not left lying unattended on a seat. While driving, these may eventually slide off the seat and drop onto the hard floor. This can often ruin a camera, lens or prism alignment.
- When in a canoe, mokoro or boat, tell your clients not to leave their equipment lying in the bottom of the vessel, as it does not take long for water to accumulate there. It may come from a dripping paddle or waves.
- Advise on the best speed of film at the appropriate time of day, or regarding the subject you are about to shoot.

- If you see people adjusting their camera lenses and then returning that hand back to the camera to push the shutter button, discreetly suggest that they keep their left hand on the lens at all times. This will stabilise the camera and will enable them the opportunity to refocus or zoom the lens instantly. The right hand will always be ready to fire off a salvo of shots at the appropriate time.
- Have beanbags available in vehicles and hides. Encourage guests to use them, as they add stability.

Offer Your Finger

There are many scenes and settings of which your guests may like to have a memory. Offer to take their camera and photograph them in the vehicle, boat, or canoe, or standing next to a massive baobab, or as a group in front of a stunning sunset, perhaps with an animal in the background (at a safe distance), or with your staff, or outside their rooms…the list is endless.

'Capture their moment'

If you are ***not*** an experienced photographer, try to frame your subjects well and don't thump the shutter button down hard, as this will cause the camera to shake and the picture will come out blurred. Always squeeze the shutter of a camera very gently after drawing in and holding your breath.

Camera Care

Africa takes its toll on many things. Modern cameras that can do everything (besides making you a cup of tea) are also quite temperamental. They can close down their operation at the slightest excuse. Your advice to your clients on the following points will help keep their equipment in as good a working order as possible.

- Be wary of ***dust;*** ensure that all cameras and lenses are well covered and protected from dust.
- Ensure all equipment is kept ***dry.*** Very few cameras, lenses, videos and binoculars are waterproof. Even if they are, it doesn't help to take risks.
- ***Clean*** binoculars and all camera equipment at least once a day. It takes five minutes and will result in better pictures from clear lenses. During these cleaning sessions, dust and dirt will be removed. An old shaving brush is an ideal tool for cleaning the outside of photographic equipment and binoculars. Don't use it on the sensitive glass of lenses and binoculars.

Hides

There are few better ways of enjoying wildlife than from a hide. Hides come in many forms. Some are built in trees, which offer panoramic views. Others are mobile and come in the shape of trailers or boats that have been positioned, adapted and camouflaged to conceal their passengers, who are also comfortable and safe.

Some of the best hides are often found underground in the structure of bunkers. From here one can enjoy all the wild visitors at ground level. These hides are often positioned very close to an attraction, often a waterhole, giving intimate experiences to those that are hidden within.

The advantages to time spent in a hide are numerous:

- Invariably they are favourably ***situated*** to view mammal or bird congregations.
- They offer the patient observer the opportunity to ***watch, enjoy*** and ***learn*** about the ***social behaviour*** of various animals as they warily approach a waterhole and interact with one another.
- When people are left in a hide for an agreed length of time, they mentally prepare themselves for their stay. They know they can't rush off from one sighting to another. They don't have a set of car keys so that they

can zoom off in a vehicle to find something more exciting. They are obliged to spend *time* studying the smaller things in life. They may be enthralled by a visit from a slender mongoose, or by the sight of an adult bateleur eagle warily scooping up water with its powerful red bill.

• Guests are given the *opportunity* to be quiet, to take in the sounds, to collect their thoughts, reflect on their experiences and to *observe.*

If you encounter the right kind of guests and you know it is safe and will be rewarding, offer to arrange for them to spend a night in a hide. It may be full moon in the driest month, when animals may come in throughout the night. Set up mattresses, mozzi nets, insect repellent, water, radio, emergency horn, a spotlight and battery. Evaluate the situation. You may want to spend the night with them to keep them informed and safe from worry. Or they may be the kind of people who might like to be on their own.

When hides are not in daily use, always ensure that they are *clean* and *safe* before guests are taken inside. Clean out dust, spider webs, bird, monkey and baboon droppings. Frogs, toads and rodents are often trapped and die in underground hides. Snakes may reside in them for their warmth.

If you leave guests in a hide, don't get distracted and forget about them, as you won't be too popular.

When working at a lodge adjoining Hwange National Park, a fellow guide dropped three young English doctors off in a tree hide in the afternoon, arranging to collect them at dusk. He subsequently forgot to collect them. Shortly after 7:30 p.m. there was a violent thunderstorm and lightening display.

To give you an idea of the ferocity of the downpour, during the storm four wildebeest had taken refuge beneath a lone acacia tree behind our house. The following morning all four lay dead beneath the tree, killed by lightening.

The young English doctors were drenched and terrified. At around 10:00 p.m. they began to walk off from the hide in an unknown direction. After an hour's walk along a firebreak, they fortunately came out at the airport and found the house belonging to the air traffic controller. They used his phone and gave the guide a bigger blast than the thunderstorm. You can imagine what it was like for him to have to go out and collect them! They were wild with anger, fear, cold and frustration.

'The unforgettable story'

Don't Forget

Finally a few rules to bear in mind:

- Don't short-change the rest of the clients in your care by favouring only those that are ultra keen on photography. Put all keen photographers in one group if possible.
- Don't take risks with expensive and sensitive equipment; be especially cautious around water.
- *Never* endanger the life of a client or any animal for the sake of the 'ultimate' photograph!

Reference Books

There are a number of great photo books available. Possibly the best and easiest to read is called *The Nature Photographer's Complete Guide to Professional Field Techniques*, written by John Shaw, a respected nature photographer based in the USA. The book will teach you all the tricks. It may be a hard book to find, but it is well worth hunting down. The publishers are American Photographic Book Publishing, or Phaidon Press in the UK.

Chapter 11

Odds and Ends

'Attempt, Persevere, Succeed.'

Burnout

No matter how dedicated you are and how much you enjoy your job, people and wildlife, make sure you don't guide for too many weeks without a break. Very few guides can keep up their genuine enthusiasm, dedication and safety when guiding for prolonged periods. In your case you may not notice it, but others will.

While many guests will tease you about your job and make out you are on one long holiday, they don't realize the stresses that come with the job, or the work that goes on behind the scenes to ensure a smooth and successful safari.

The biggest of these hidden pressures is being with a variety of people, of all ages, cultures and societies for sixteen hours a day, thirty days a week, four weeks a month without respite. They bring you their wants, needs and desires. You are on show and there is a silent pressure on you to 'produce the goods'. On top of this all is the length you have to go to ensure their safety, comfort and happiness. As a teacher, you have a new class enrolling every few days. During this time you must educate them and show all that your little patch of Africa has to offer. This often involves repeating yourself in some way with each new set of guests.

New guests will ask you the same questions: Where do you come from? How long have you worked at this particular camp? Where were you before? Your wife, children, brothers, parents? etc., only to ask the same questions again the following day having forgotten that you bared all only hours before.

You will have remained calm and bitten your lip, without drawing blood, when asked for the umpteenth time that year to identify your most common and vocal bird. After four days with the same group you will still be asked by someone to identify an animal, which happens to be a waterbuck, and was seen three times on each safari activity by that same person.

You have been rubbing shoulders, daily, with the camp staff for eight weeks, heard all the same old gripes, grumbles, cutting remarks, whining, whingeing and moaning. You have put out a hundred fires behind the scenes, juggled safari activities to fit in with vehicle breakdowns, fixed loos that don't flush, showers with no hot water, temperamental boat engines, water pumps and boreholes, driven all night to the closest town to get an emergency supply of rations, ice, drinks or fuel, listened to the standard sob story from staff who have to go out unexpectedly because of the death of a 'brother'(and sent them off) operating an understaffed camp without letting the clients see the cracks. You have had to deal with an obnoxious national parks game scout but have kept your cool. You have waited at the airstrip for hours for an aircraft that was meant to land 'at any time'.

All such scenarios and many more come with the job. You owe it to yourself and, most importantly, to your clients, to take days off at least every eight weeks, twelve at a push. You need this break to recharge your batteries, and to have a change of scenery and people.

Often you will come back from your time off, exasperated with the stresses of the town or city that you visited and so appreciative of your workplace. You will

'Burnout'

be fired up to be back in familiar surroundings and to see some of the animals you have come to know from constant observation. You can't wait to take your next guests out, or even to listen to the same old moans from a certain staff member.

Burnout is just as easy to get 500 kilometres away from a city. You don't have to be a high-powered business executive to succumb it, it is one of life's natural occurrences.

I was making my way through a spate of 13 back-to-back safaris, the shortest being a duration of four nights. I was on my tenth safari with an enthusiastic group of South Africans with whom I had safaried on a number of occasions. One of them was a doctor, who had all the vibrancy, compassion and wisdom you could ever ask for in a person!

The two of us were retracing our tracks one morning, looking for a pair of lost sunglasses. He asked me in a casual and friendly manner if I had ever heard of 'executive burnout'? I replied in the negative, intimating that I wasn't an executive and was therefore immune to burnout! I thought to myself, 'How could I ever show burnout? I had learnt over the years to cope with any repetition that comes with guiding, and with long hours and continual people pressure. Surely I wasn't showing the effects of the past seven weeks, especially with an appreciative, easy-going group like this?'

It took a good friend like him to make me wake up to the fact that as guides we can't keep up the same energy and positive output in our work over a prolonged period without a break. In the end you will only be fooling yourself and short-changing your clients.

I have seen guide-burnout quite often in guides who have over-committed themselves. They often have blank stares, no more lively twinkle in the eye, a tired and false laugh, and show signs of apathy, boredom and disinterest.

There are 5 stages to burnout:

Enthusiasm becomes **Stagnation**...
Stagnation slowly evolves into **Frustration**...
which then develops into **Apathy** ......resulting in **Burnout**!

The aim is to stop and break the cycle. This is obviously easier to do the sooner it is done i.e. it is easier to break at stagnation than at the apathy stage.

There are a few ways to prevent Bush Burnout:
- Physical exercise. Personal time in a safari camp is extremely limited. The last thing you want to do when you do have some time to yourself is to break into a full sweat from strenuous exercises like jogging, stationary exercise bike, lifting weights, etc. Having a fit body, however, will get you through a lot in life.
- Good diet. Not an easy thing to maintain, when eating large safari meals three times a day. This is where you need strong self-discipline. Don't have three big meals and desserts each day. Eat as much fruit as possible. Drink large quantities of water.
- Weed out relationships that are draining. Avoid negative people wherever possible.
- Nourish your mind through involvement in hobbies or a special interest, maybe photography, botany, ornithology, or a particular animal or species.
- Introduce variety into your workday wherever possible.
- We all have limits, and you must maintain realistic expectations of yourself.
- Do take your days off. Don't impress your boss by showing how dedicated you are and how many months in a row you can work. Change your environment when you take time off or go on leave.

When you eventually own your own safari camp, or manage a number of guides, don't work all the spark and fire out of them. This is easy to do in the busy months of high season; just one more week with its financial rewards. A monetary carrot won't make them guide any better. It's the physical, mental and emotional pressure over extended periods that eventually takes its toll.

Ensure you have sufficient guides for the season. Take into account time off and possible sickness from malaria or injury. Correct staffing levels will alleviate constant pressure on your guides, which will allow them to guide creatively and naturally. By knowing the limits of your staff and arranging their time off wisely, you will give your customers a far better wildlife experience and ensure the most important factor of all - their safety!

Female Guides

For centuries, hunting and wildlife guiding has been a male dominated occupation. There are a few notable and hardy women who have been exceptional pioneers and hunters and whose names have entered the pages of African history.

The past two decades has seen more women entering the guiding profession,

'The female of the species'

often showing up their male counterparts. Women guides know that the odds are stacked against them and that everyone is watching to see whether they will put a foot wrong.

Those women who survive the initial difficulties of their guiding careers often become excellent guides. Unlike men they are not ego driven. Since their testosterone levels are lower, they are able to put all their energy into their guiding skills. Women tend to be better at remembering information gleaned from personal observation, and seem to learn better from other guides and books. Women guides tend to be more compassionate about wildlife, and often exude more feeling for the subject. They are also more aware of their client's needs and discomfort.

Being a female guide in Africa is not easy. It is difficult for them to earn full respect from junior staff. With a culture in Africa where men don't easily take orders from women, they have this handicap to over come. They need to be competent in changing flat tyres of various safari vehicles, by using a highlift jack and placing heavy and cumbersome spare wheels in place; and they need to carry out vehicle repairs in emergencies. Other challenges include driving competently in heavy sand and thick mud, using a winch, being able to shoot accurately and confidently with a heavy calibre rifle while ensuring the safety of their guests but still giving them a close-up, wildlife experience. They need to remain calm under life-threatening conditions, and show no signs of fear or panic. Unfortunately, they are in the spotlight a lot more than men.

Most guests can't believe that a woman can walk and protect them among all the legendary wild animals of Africa. On a number of occasions I have seen an aircraft disgorge its occupants at a bush airstrip, and have observed the startled faces of the passengers when they were met by a woman guide, tanned legs extending from under a pair of khaki shorts, a wide brimmed hat, a thin arm offering a hand of welcome before they set of on a four-day walking safari.

The male clients clearly had their doubts about this fair maiden being able to protect them from charging lion or elephant. It won't do for the male ego to have a woman protecting them from the wilds of Africa. Their wives looked on in disbelief, with the thought of their husbands following those shapely brown legs down all the game trails.

If you are a male guide, don't turn your nose up at female guides and underestimate them. Your clients may have been out on a safari with both you and your female contemporary. How would you and your ego feel if they were to request her as their guide for the rest of their stay?

The top women guides in Africa are well aware of their new guests' initial surprise and apprehension. It takes only a few hours for the clients to see the true calibre of their lady guide. They then enjoy her company and often become good friends.

A group of clients once gave me the following comparison between their female guide (who worked very much in the shadow of a well-known and charismatic professional guide) and the male guide himself:

They said their male guide was like a tube of toothpaste, who needed to be squeezed before he gave out information.

The female guide was likened to a bag of sugar with a small hole at the bottom, always giving out small amounts of pleasing information.

As in any industry it is really up to each individual as to how he or she feels about him or herself and how motivated a person is to excel in this work. It's a question of how much time and dedication they are prepared to put in to be proficient and professional at what they do.

If you are a woman and want to become a guide, don't be put off if it is portrayed as a job best suited to the opposite sex. Be assured, your work will be cut out for you.

Remember the great motto of: attempt, ***persevere,*** succeed. It is the middle word that takes time, energy, endurance and heartache, but if you can persevere you will find it worth while in the long run.

Freelance Guides

As a rule, freelance guides don't work for any one employer on a permanent basis. The freelancer has a sense of independence and self-employment, which can, however, backfire when tourism slumps.

Freelancers will try to book up around 200 guiding days each year with one or (more often) a number of safari operators. This affords them the opportunity to work in a variety of habitats. Different kinds of contract can be drawn up between the guide and operator. The most common is for a set daily rate, and often requires the operator to go to the expense of getting them in and out of the safari area. Adequate accommodation must be provided, and obviously all meals and drinks come with the job.

Freelancers work quite hard during the season, and then spend the rest of the year holidaying on various continents around the world and enjoying the hospitality offered by some of the valuable contacts they have made over the years. Some guides will use this time to broaden their horizons by exploring other parks in Africa, South America, India, etc. Those guides with families will spend the off-season making up time as a spouse and parent.

Although life as a freelancer sounds glamorous to the full-time guide who possibly earns the same amount of money as the freelancer, but over an eleven-month period, there are a number of downsides to life as a freelance guide.

Freelancers are usually contracted only when an operator is so busy that there aren't enough of their own guides available, or if a full-time guide with the appropriate qualifications is not there to step in.

When the bottom falls out of the tourist industry (as can happen so quickly in Africa), there is little or no work for freelance guides. They can go from a situation in good times, where they can virtually name their daily rate and conditions, to dropping their fee by more than half, with only a few safari days for the season. During lean times (often caused by political instability) they seek employment in neighbouring countries. Here they will face work permit hassles and have a feeling of 'not belonging'. They will have built up a name in their own country, but since they are not necessarily well known in neighbouring countries, they don't enjoy the same respect and freedom they knew in their home country.

At the beginning of the new millennium, Zimbabwe was bracing for yet another busy year in tourism. A few months later there was an escalation in pre-election violence, which triggered a stream of cancellations from international tour operators and their clients. Almost all freelancers were soon without work. Safari companies had to cancel most freelancer contracts because of the 'situation' (as it became known) and began to reluctantly lay off full-time staff so as to keep their businesses afloat. Those companies that didn't close down kept only their long-standing employees wherever possible because of a history with the company and in return for their loyalty in the past. Freelancers invariably didn't have these advantages.

Early in the year a certain professional guide was dictating guiding rates and conditions to a well-respected safari company. They couldn't agree on terms. The freelancer found other work under the desired conditions and phoned up the operations director of the original safari company, to gloat over the new contract and basically telling him where to go...

A few months later, with bookings down to a trickle, the freelancer, now without any firm guiding days, eventually settled for work with a very mediocre safari company at a third of the original daily rate.

While freelance guides enjoy a lot of freedom and have fewer camp responsibilities than full-time guides, they don't have the same sense of permanence and feeling of security. A number of permanent guides have homes with 'character' close to the camp where they work, with their worldly possessions around them: their natural history book collections, slides, paintings and personal memorabilia.

Some companies will offer their full-time guides medical aid and a pension scheme. Some safari companies may have numerous camps scattered around the country as well as in neighbouring countries. Their full-time guides will often work at various camps, and get to know new habitats and animals. On time off or leave, they can enjoy the freedom of their sister camps. Most of all, they have a sense of belonging.

There are some down-sides to safari companies employing freelance guides.

Very few freelancers will give the company the same degree of loyalty and commitment as a permanent employee.

Not many freelance guides like to get their hands dirty and muck in with the menial work behind the scenes. Some have an attitude of 'I am here to guide and that's all that I am prepared to do'.

If the food is bad, the vehicle breaks down or game viewing is poor, these guides will often make excuses to distance themselves from that particular safari operation. They may come up with statements like, 'I am only here helping out for a few weeks because the last guide up and left all of a sudden' or 'I normally work in Buggamazoo National Park for Bambazonkie Safaris. You should see all the animals there! And the food, it's the best I have ever eaten! Their vehicles are all brand new, I've never had a breakdown. Last week when I was freelancing for them, I watched the "Big Five" three times in a day!'

'It's not my job'

Some freelance guides can actually introduce a negative impact on a safari operation. They may suggest competitor camps for the guest's next visit. A number of freelancers have their own little companies and safari operations and will occasionally encourage camp clients to book with them next time round.

Freelancers often don't have the rapport and good relationship with the back-up staff, especially when things begin to go wrong on a safari. Without an intimate knowledge of how things work behind the scenes, poor decisions can be made which may cost the clients precious safari time and give an impression of inefficiency.

There are freelance guides who, although they earn a high daily rate, expect the vehicle or boat to been cleaned, filled with fuel, and have the cooler box and snacks loaded. After the safari activity, the vehicle or boat is left for some nameless soul to take care of. Some guides will arrive the day an 'expedition' safari begins.

This may be a mobile camping safari, walking or canoeing trail. They come in with backpack and rifle, meet their clients and set off, expecting everything to have been organised beforehand. They have not checked the equipment, food, drinks, ice, fuel etc.

Freelance guides will seldom know an area as well as full-time resident guides. This will mean that the clients don't get to see all that an area can offer. Freelancers may not have a longstanding relationship and understanding with the local national parks authorities, which is an advantage when problems occur.

Despite the above, there are a few very dedicated and professional freelance guides. They are discreet and loyal to the companies to which they are contracted. These guides are seldom without work.

Freelancer Hints

- Be loyal and dedicated to each safari company that hires you.
- Wear the uniform of the camp you work for.
- When about to embark on an 'expedition' safari, come in at least a day early. You will get a feel for the area, you can tune in to the bird calls, and familiarise yourself with the local plants.
- Check all the equipment, drinks, food, ice, etc., as this will avoid awkward situations once the safari is under way. Although you may apportion the blame elsewhere, it won't change the fact that the paying guests will be inconvenienced. Get to know your back-up crew.
- If you are a hunter for most of the year and obtain freelance work at a tourist lodge, don't discuss your main occupation.
- Offer your help behind the scenes at the camp that has hired you. It will help pass time and give you a feeling of belonging. The staff and management will respect you for it. You may be in great demand when tourism is booming, but you never know who you may need when tourism slumps.
- Never poach staff from a camp that has hired you. You may have a close relationship with camp A who are looking for a chef, waiter, driver, etc. While working at camp B on a freelance basis you meet just the person for the job. Don't even think of getting involved in this type of underhand behaviour. It will all come out in the end. Don't burn the bridges in your profession.
- Don't forget who is hiring you. Refrain from promoting yourself or another safari operation.

'The conservationist'

Other Than Guiding

I have listened to guides discussing who might be the best guide in the area, country, etc. They generally rate a guide according to his or her immense knowledge, with the 'best' guide having the **combined** knowledge of Smithers, Roberts and Coates Palgrave.

Seldom do they take into account the most important factors in guiding: Genuinely enjoying people and understanding *all* their needs and wants, and being able to put over the big picture with the right amount of knowledge, at the right time and in plain, simple English.

No mention is made of what these 'guiding gurus' do for wildlife conservation when they are not being paid to guide. How many guides go back to their communities and give of their free time to the promotion of wildlife and wild areas? How many give talks and slide shows to schools, old-age homes, orphanages, hospitals, farming communities, wildlife and natural history societies? How many take school children on outings to local wildlife sanctuaries or private game farms?

How much time and effort do *you* put in to the community on wildlife awareness? Your job isn't only about tourism, a salary, profit and time off.

You are in a fortunate position of having an extremely valuable commodity to share with your fellow man. It doesn't always have to be for financial gain. There are those that can't afford to come out on safari, so share some of your exciting experiences with them. These accounts can be enhanced by video, slides, photo albums and written stories.

You are a custodian of nature, a believer in conservation. Use your talents generously and wisely.

Enjoy

You have chosen a career that can be personally rewarding while offering you a healthy outdoor life and exposure to the greatest volume and diversity of animals on earth. You have the opportunity to share all of this with your fellow man, to give them once-in-a-lifetime experiences, to build lifelong friendships, and to play a part in the conservation of wild areas and all they contain. You have the opportunity to watch and learn from all that nature has to offer. You are a teacher in the biggest and best-stocked classroom ever imaginable, always changing its lessons and pupils.

Be proud of what you do. Never lose sight of the main purpose of guiding. Give the most important people in your industry their money's worth. Help to realize their dreams and fantasies about this great continent. Allay their fears, share your knowledge and be genuine in all that you say and do.

Most of all, be aware of their safety at all times.

Enjoy one of the most privileged occupations on earth!

Chapter 12

From the Horse's Mouth

*'The difference between ordinary and
extraordinary is that little extra'*

The book has nearly come to an end. On your safaris always save the best for last and always try to end on a climax. So often in guiding we encounter an amazing wildlife spectacle in the middle of a safari, and the guests will be bowled over by the experience. It is so easy to think then that we have completed our work and can freewheel from there on for the remainder of the trip, often even reminding the guests how extremely fortunate they were to experience such an event!

*The last 24 hours with your guests are
the most important of the entire safari.*

Keep them entertained and happy. Show them you haven't lost momentum and enthusiasm. Surprise them with a special treat on the last day. This may be a private bush dinner next to their favourite waterhole, an extended game drive, a farewell cake made of elephant dung, covered with icing. Ensure you always have a real cake to follow this up , once the playful joke has been realized. The list of things you can conjure up to make them feel extra special is endless. Don't forget the difference between an *ordinary* guide and an *extraordinary* guide is that little five lettered word, *'extra'*!

Extra time, extra effort, extra enthusiasm, extra dedication, extra smile, all equals extra happy guests!

This final chapter contains extracts from letters I have received from people who have been on safari to Africa in the past. I requested various African tour operators from all parts of the world to ask their clients what their expectations were of their safari guide, before coming out on safari. I also asked them to comment on their impressions after the safari.

So, here you have it right from the horse's mouth. The dreams, aspirations, expectations, wants, needs, joys, feelings, desires, thoughts, hopes and wishes from a small collection of people that have helped to keep our industry alive. These people have made our governments realize the need to keep vast tracts of wilderness open, as a way of attracting large sums of foreign currency. These folks have helped pay our salaries, to clothe, feed and educate our children and last, but not least, they have given us one of the most rewarding outdoor professions on this planet!

These are the true life feelings and aspirations, not from a guide like you or me, but from the people that we serve, our clients and guests.

Question: What does a traveller expect from a safari guide?

1. In my opinion, the world! A good guide makes sure everyone comes back alive. A great guide can tell where everyone's comfort level is and challenge them while still ensuring everyone is having a good time. A great guide has stories to tell, knowledge to share and a personality that conveys leadership when it's needed but fades into a supporting role when the group is developing those bonds that make for lifelong friendships. When I think about the best trips I have taken, there was usually an exceptional guide involved.
Carol Patterson, Alberta, USA

2. I believe a guide must be friendly and affable. He must have good communicating skills and really be a friend of his clients. With the knowledge that a guide's position is one of 'service', he has to be able to put his client ahead of himself. If he has this service attitude, I am sure he will get it right.

We all know that there is no place for the big macho-type image in a guide. Most of the clients are big deals anyway - otherwise they wouldn't be able to afford coming on these sort of trips - and they will see through a young fellow who is trying to ruffle his feathers and show how important and what a big deal he is. That is probably one of the biggest put offs. Obviously, the chap has to have a good knowledge of his area and what he is guiding. He must be enthusiastic about this and knowledgeable - and he must also have a reasonable knowledge of first aid, vehicle maintenance, radio communication, firearm etiquette, etc.

He must have the ability to change his plan or route as necessary and the sensitivity to tailor his guiding to his particular group. He must also be able to listen - clients want to tell their stories too. With that, he must be able to display a wide range of interests. But the enthusiasm about his job will quickly become evident to any client, and you can't be a good guide without being enthusiastic!
Haggis Black, Adelaide, South Africa

3. Our experience has been that a confident, friendly, outgoing personality is almost as important as a guide's knowledge of the wildlife and the bush. I think this applies particularly on longer trips, when clients are spending quite a few days in the sole company of the guide. It's all very well for the guide to have a fantastic knowledge of the plants and animals, but he also needs to be a communicator. A guide who can communicate his knowledge well will keep clients interested in what it going on around them, whether they see a lot of game or not.

The guide should also be a leader, the social cement of the group as it were, bringing different types of personalities together. A group can be made up of such varied personalities, with different backgrounds and interests, and it isn't always easy to get them to 'bond' together. But this can make the difference between a great trip and an ordinary one. The guide must attempt to include everyone in the group, and not ignore the quieter or less likeable clients. To try and cater for the disparate interests, and also set the pace to the slowest, or oldest, (whilst trying to avoid the more active members getting bored - not easy!). Clients also need to have confidence in a guide's knowledge of the bush and his ability to handle dangerous or difficult situations, such as an animal attack, an injury or a vehicle breakdown. I've often noticed how, when things go wrong, a confident, well-liked guide who has the trust of the group will steer through any problems fairly easily, and the clients will see it all as part of the adventure. In contrast, a very reserved guide (particularly if he can't speak the clients' language very well) may have trouble keeping the group happy and they are more likely to complain afterwards. We find this happens more often in East Africa, where the clients have a guide who doesn't speak English very well. If the safari goes well and the clients see lots of game, everything will be fine. But if the safari has problems or the vehicle breaks down, the clients are far more likely to feel that they are in some sort of danger, or that the safari operator is incompetent, or has badly maintained vehicles, rather than see it as part of a typical safari. Though I remember a Kenyan driver/guide we had once who got sick of the constant problems, jumped out of the truck and ran off, never to return. Naturally it also helps if the guide is a bit of a raconteur - able to entertain clients with stories of the bush and keep a conversation going at mealtimes. Not a showman necessarily, but a friendly, easy personality. Then again some eccentric personalities also make good guides - if not the best! So in our experience clients can have a good time on safari even if they don't see that much game, and even if something does go wrong, as long as they have a guide who makes the trip interesting and ensures the group works well as a whole. A remarkable knowledge of the animals, birds, plants local folklore etc. is obviously the great advantage of any guide. Not only does it make a safari more interesting and keep clients entertained, but a good guide should give his clients a better understanding of the whole ecosystem that surrounds them. They will then feel that they have learned something of value and have a better appreciation of the world around them. Their trip will become more than just a holiday, but a profoundly personal experience that they will remember forever, and of course want to rediscover once again in the future! I hope this has been of some help. It does sound rather idealistic, but I'm speaking generally. I have to say that most of the best guides we've been on

safari with have been rather eccentric characters and lacking in a couple of the qualities mentioned above! But who wants perfection?

Sara Cameron

Steve Cameron's addition's: The guide needs to identify the sorts of experiences his clients might want, for example, with a guide who inspires confidence some clients might be happy to get really close to dangerous animals, such as elephants. Different clients might panic and complain that their guide is irresponsible. Guides shouldn't feel inhibited by clients who think they know it all or who have been to Africa lots of times. They should still go ahead and give lots of information - in fact it's a good opportunity for them to go into even more detail about things like insects, geology, bush lore etc. A guide should feel free to give their own interpretations of things rather than just give a textbook view, but certainly qualify it that the observation is their own personal view, which may be in contrast to other established views.

Sara and Steve Cameron, African Wildlife Safaris, South Melbourne, Australia

4. There are probably three basic reasons why someone wants to go on safari in Africa. For some, possibly even the majority, it is a once-in-a-lifetime trip and is unlikely to be repeated. For them it is usually the animals that are the main attraction. Then there are those at the opposite extreme who have a particular interest such as ornithology, botany, the big cats etc., and they require highly specialized knowledge from their guide. In the middle are those who are probably the main users of professional guides, and they are those for whom the animals are 'the gilt on the gingerbread,' but the gingerbread itself is the wilderness, the primeval nature of the bush, desert or veldt, and the magic of being, if only for a few days in a world untouched by man. It is important that the guide knows what bracket his client falls into.

The most obvious attribute that one expects from a guide is a wide-ranging knowledge of the flora and fauna of the area. His ability to track, to observe, to explain and to teach is taken for granted. What differentiates a good guide from an outstanding guide are other attributes in addition to these basic ones.

Those who are prepared to pay the additional costs of a safari run by a professional guide are usually those who have been to Africa before and have been captivated by it. They are also likely to be widely traveled and to be fairly affluent. They will expect efficiency. They should not expect luxury but they should expect all the arrangements to work smoothly, for vehicles and tents to be well maintained, for staff to be polite, happy and capable. In short, they expect to be looked after by a well run and well lead team.

Enthusiasm is an essential element in a good guide. It transmits itself to clients and makes a world of difference. It can make even warthog droppings interesting! He or she should be sensitive to the aspects of the land or wildlife, that which interests the clients and that which does not.

A good guide will be easy to talk to, patient with stupid questions, and able to converse, both on drives and at meals, on subjects other than the flora and fauna.

A guide who knows where to position a vehicle to obtain the best light and composition for a good photograph can make a world of difference. Photographs are usually the only tangible evidence of a safari and good ones are an advertisement for the guide and his country.

He should have a natural way with children. On our first visit to the Okavango there were two families with five children in their early teens. Our guide divided his time equally with the vehicle between the children and us adults. The children were captivated and have never forgotten the experience he gave them of Africa at its best. He fascinated them by showing them what could be learnt from warthog droppings. The guide should remember that the children are the next generation of those who will keep his profession in business!

It should be obvious to the client that their guide has a deep and genuine love for the country and its wildlife. He should know its history, its geography and its geology.

It is essential that one's guide has a natural, relaxed, and genuinely friendly relationship with the natives of the country who help him or her make a safari a success. Of even more importance, it should be clear to his clients that he respects the natives, their culture, customs and traditions and is not patronizing towards them.

It may be a difficult and sensitive subject but if not dealt with sensibly it can cause problems. With reference to tipping. I expect the guide to tell me what is a typical level for tipping his staff. As far as his tip is concerned I would expect him to let the tour operator have some ideas of the bracket before leaving on safari.

Finally the guide should remember that a good word-of-mouth testimonial from his clients when they get back home is probably worth at least as much as all the spending on advertising.

Richard Todd, Hampshire, UK

5. Our experience with guided tours prior to Africa included fully guided trips to China and the Copper Canyon in Mexico. In both cases the guides were knowledgeable, helpful and interesting. In China, we were excessively controlled and felt restricted due to the political nature of the country. Our guide in Mexico was more of an organizer and translator than an actual guide. Prior to leaving for Zimbabwe, we expected the guides to be concerned primarily with our safety and comfort. We were pleasantly surprised at the depth of knowledge the guides demonstrated about all aspects of the fauna and flora in each region we visited. Along with their knowledge, they were very friendly, courteous and fun to be with. Obviously the guide-training program in Zimbabwe is thorough, professional and successful.

While on a walk we encountered a breeding herd of elephants, our guide was able to position our group to keep us downwind and quiet so that we could observe the feeding habits of this herd in their natural environment for a considerable period of time at very close range. His experience and knowledge gave all of us a feeling of confidence and dispelled any notion of danger. We felt this was a particularly interesting and exciting experience. Another experience that stands out in our minds occurred at with a guide at Ruckomechi Camp. When we first met him he questioned us on what we had seen to date and what we would still like to see in the time remaining. Lions and leopards were our unanimous choice. Without hesitation, he focused on this request and concentrated on finding a pride of lions known to be in the area. He organized the group to search for the pride and although it had not been spotted for three or four days, we found them in two to three hours. We spent the next hour in close proximity to the pride and then found them again the following morning. We were able to follow them as they ranged out to hunt.

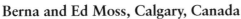

Berna and Ed Moss, Calgary, Canada

6. He or she should:
   a. Be aware of age and limitations of group; e.g. hard of hearing, need to urinate more frequently, difficulty getting in and out of vehicles.
   b. As the result of a bad experience in the past, clarify if water in vehicles is for the group or just driver and guide?
   c. Recognize special needs of those with camcorders and fancy cameras versus those who just want to view animals and take usual photos.
   d. Separate smokers from non-smokers.
   e. Try to be available, at least occasionally, during rest times for individual clients who'd like to ask questions but won't ask during 'competitive' talking.

Katrina and Marshall Clark, USA

7. I can think of one example near the beginning of our safari experience. Maybe a little briefing from the guide when you first arrive at a camp would prepare us better. We had no really up close and personal experiences at our camp in the Matobo region so when we hit Makalolo Camp in Hwange we were rank novices. Some of us had read about elephant behaviour, i.e. mock charging, but when it happens on your first night as you are walking nonchalantly back after dinner to your elevated tent with the guide leading the way, wow! We heard first and then saw (in the pitch black with only the guides flashlight to spot him) a wonderful huge bull elephant ripping grass and eating it. We were also at eye level. At the moment that he mock charged, we were ready to run, whichever way even though we had read to do the opposite. We got a firm set of instructions at that moment and in hindsight, probably would have needed a reminder anyway at the precise moment. However we were all huddled behind our guide, not breathing! When the elephant went back to munching we, under our guides direction, started moving slowly along again. Again he mock charged and our performance was repeated. Needless to say, it is a moment none of us will forget, but a set of expectations on arrival may have prepared us better.
Sandy McMeekin, Canada.

8. Thoughts on Guides:
• Ask occasionally of a client regarding his/her expectations, etc., and even inquire of their background.
• Mix with all members of the group.
• Try not to stay out all night on the night drives. Ask, for some may be tired.
• Provide drinking water for long hot drives and blankets for cold ones.
• Speak up - many guides are too softly spoken.

   I don't like guides with a 'tude. (That's American slang for attitude and not complimentary.) These guides bothered me because they were either cocky or condescending. Guides need to get to know their clients to determine how much knowledge they have of wildlife. I can't tell you how many times I've been told about the number of bones in a giraffe's neck - and sounding like a memorized spiel straight out of the textbook. I must admit that's far more common in East Africa than Southern.
Nancy Cherry, Kansas, USA

9. We have found that excellence in guiding depends more on plain old personality than anything else. I compare 'the perfect guide' to building a house. Obviously, skill and knowledge of how to keep your guests feeling comfortable and safe is the foundation. Skill in interpreting natural history is the framework. Guests want to know about the environment they're in, and if you can share information in an interesting way that relates to them, that's fabulous. Eric and I still talk about how impressed we were on our 1990 trip: our guide could just pick up a piece of anything on the ground and tell us something amazing about it. But the finishing of the house, the real magic boils down to the question: are you a fun person to be with? Do you have a sense of humour? Are you enthusiastic about what you're doing? Do you have conversational skills above and beyond natural history interpretation? I remember canoeing down the Zambezi, and our guide asked us about the Quebec problem in Canada. We again were impressed, as he took an interest in something in our country. We could discuss it, and then quickly switch to watching an elephant doing something interesting on the riverbank, which our guide would explain to us. It is this combination that makes the best guide.
Sue and Eric Webb, Alberta, Canada

10. My requirements are for a guide to have a superb and detailed knowledge of the local wildlife and its movements resulting in the opportunity of seeing animals performing in the wild without the knowledge (if possible) of human presence. I would expect to be as close to the wildlife without disturbing their activities, together with explanations as to the reasons behind their behaviour. A good guide should also be able to explain the terrain. Natural vegetation and the climatic conditions that affect the existence of the resident human population and the animals and birds in the wild. Added to this would be the  opportunity to savour a beautiful sunrise or view or sound at a particular time of day as well as any local custom or occasion that may be taking place among the inhabitants of the area or country being visited. These experiences all add to a greater enjoyment and understanding of Africa. All of this would have to be executed with professionalism but not so much so that the opportunity of the unexpected event is removed or the spirit of adventure is lost. It goes without saying that the more exclusivity in terms of being the only humans present is important.
Sue Jackson-Stops, Northampton, UK

11. We needed them to be good with people - to be friendly, have a good sense of humour and patient (since so many of us were city people from Canada - what do we know about canoeing down the Zambezi?). We lived with our guides all day, from an early-morning rising in the dark to a late-night departure for our beds in the dark. If we had a grouchy guide, it would not have been a happy experience. I remember one of our guides, playing a trick on us on one of our walks that just had us all laughing like crazy. We found out that the depth and breadth of their knowledge about plants, trees, animals, birds, geography, history and the tribes in the areas (and in one case our guide, knew all about the stars, for heavens' sake!) it was mind boggling. Every day we were constantly learning about all aspects of the African environment that surrounded us. We needed our guides to be forever on their guard without us knowing - while we were eating a leisurely lunch on the river, little were we aware that their rifles were still within reach 'just in case'. Sad to say, guides really need experience in how to successfully shoot large animals - it wasn't needed on our trip but it may be one day. We found more than one poet among the guides - their verbal descriptions of what was right in front of us painted a more complete picture than just the visual and increased our appreciation immensely.

They needed that extra 'sense' of when the 'tourists' might be in trouble, e.g., my husband had not experienced river canoeing with a conflicting wind and the first day on the Zambezi, with just two of us in the canoe, we had some difficulties. The next day, with no fanfare, we had a guide in the back of the canoe and we were then free to enjoy being on the river for days without the previous day's struggle. We needed the guides to give us a close encounter of the elephant kind without getting us into trouble - they need to know the animals' tolerance to people. We had amazing drives at Makalolo where we were surrounded by elephants – our guide really knew where to park that jeep for our sundowners. We canoed side-by-side with a beautiful and tolerant elephant across a channel of the Zambezi. Our guide, said 'no need to paddle, just enjoy'. A large, perfect picture of that elephant and that moment in time is on my wall today. The guides know that these crazy tourists need to eat and drink every 2 hours in order to be kept in good working order - we had so much food I put on 6 lbs. on the trip. The life of a guide is so extremely different from the lives of the tourists who usually spend their working days in high-rise office towers in big cities. But they take us to their world with immense wisdom, humour and the best, wild stories we have ever heard by a fire at night - and then they send us back to our office towers all in one piece and dying to go back one day to see our friends once more.

Pat, Canada

12. There are many things required of a guide. Some are obvious, such as: stable character, fitness, health, friendliness, knowledgeability, responsibility. There are also some less obvious requirements.

On occasions I have been aware of some minor problems. These have included:

a. Lack of knowledge on the requirements for good still photography. I feel that all guides should have a firm understanding of lighting, positioning, and photographic opportunity. Some of our safaris have been led by keen photographers, and this has been a great advantage, particularly since one of the reasons that we choose to visit Africa is for photography. A good guide should be able to help experienced as well as inexperienced photographers.

b. Lack of understanding of the requirements for good video footage. Many guides have not even known that a video camera records sound! I have videos spoiled by constant nattering of guides (often in a local dialect, and often on the two way radio) when lions are roaring, elephants are trumpeting, and birds are calling.

c. Favoritism of some clients, to the neglect of others. Sally and I have always been very well looked after on every safari. However I have noted on a few occasions that one or two clients were neglected in conversations, or not included in decision making.

d. Eagerness to quickly leave an interesting animal sighting, to go searching for something else.

e. Inability to empathise with the requirements of everyone when on a walking safari. The speed and distance covered while walking should always be kept within the limits of the slowest walker, and the least fit client. I have witnessed people in tears because of the pace and certainly not enjoying themselves, While the guide was totally unaware and following close on the heels of the tracker- both doing their own SAS safari.

Having said that Sally and I hold Africa as our favourite holiday destination, and have enjoyed a fabulous time during every trip to Africa.

Ron Woody, Mosman, Australia

13. What I seek from a guide is knowledge of their area, both flora and fauna, especially fauna. I also respect that no one can know absolutely everything, and I find it refreshing when someone actually admits to not knowing, but goes to various sources to find out. On our last trip to Kenya and Zambia,

most of the trip was excellent but we were frustrated with our guide in Kenya who tended to BS his way through an awful lot of country. The world changed when he drove the bus back and we spent one day with United Touring's head guide in the Masai Mara. Here was a man who intensely loved the country and the animals, especially rhinos and was full of knowledge and enthusiasm. The other major concern I had in Kenya was the entire lack of concern for the environment. We only needed to see a group of vans around something and we were barrelling across the Savannah to join the group. One particularly sad incident was our first sighting of a young leopard in a tree during daylight. The vans were driving around the tree and tearing up the bush.

In Zambia we had excellent guides and great experiences. So, in a nutshell what I expect is knowledge, enthusiasm and enough humility to admit not knowing, but to find out.
Marguerite Paulsen, Canada

14. Our safari was enhanced by a guide who enthusiastically accompanied us throughout, knowledgeably answered all our questions, teaching us to look around us as we walked and not at our feet, mixed rushes of adrenaline with learning to appreciate and relish the solitude and the solemnity of the bush, told stories and anecdotes of Africa when suitable moments arose and with sufficient authority, he kept the children under his spell and in doing so allowed me to totally relax and enjoy a holiday of a lifetime.
Trina Mc Mullen, UK

15. I'm not sure what I expected when I took my trip, but I do know that I was absolutely bowled over by all the guides. I particularly appreciated their depth of knowledge about the area, including animals, plants, trees, birds and - what an amazing bonus - stars. Because of the plethora of great wildlife programs on TV these days, a lot of people are somewhat knowledgeable so I think the guides can add a lot to the experience by providing personal stories and anecdotes. I also felt completely safe, and I think this is important. I'm not an especially nervous person, but it's reassuring to feel that the guide knows exactly what he/she is doing. I dislike guns intensely (about as intensely as I love wildlife), so it was good to know that they were there as a last resort, and that guide's knowledge, experience and common sense were our best defence. I also appreciated the fact that the guides deliberately

split up their groups so that our safari vehicles weren't behaving like bumper cars. Everyone had a superb experience without tripping all over one another.

In more general terms, I was extremely impressed by their overall courtesy and friendliness (as opposed to familiarity). I would say that a good guide needs to strike a balance between professionalism and the charm of a good host. Since everyone is different, with different expectations, I expect they need to gauge each individual and respond accordingly. For the most part, I found the guides were able to do this and, consequently, enjoyed some very interesting conversations on a wide range of topics. Like any good communicators, they need to be as good at listening as they are at talking about what they know. Oh, and a sense of humour is essential - for anyone!
Margaret Sparkes, Calgary, Canada

16. Not to be critical, the guides we had in Kenya in 1983 treated our safari as a job, which it was. They would answer questions, but really didn't have any passion for their work or the area where they lived. They seldom offered information or observations on their own initiative.

A guide must be knowledgeable about the area, but he/she must know the group they are guiding: what their interests and expectations are. They need to know the flora and fauna of the area, but should know the people of the area, the customs and the history. Since the people on these safaris are already knowledgeable and know quite a bit about the animals that they will encounter. For other groups, animal identification may be enough and that is where the guide needs to be able to judge his/her audience and structure the day's activity accordingly. I know in Africa we saw lots of animals and our guide was able to name them all, but he never related any stories about them. They were just animals.  Yet our guide in Australia, who had worked in the Outback and knew a lot about the animals, the people and the land, was able to tell stories, that made the trip enjoyable and memorable. This sharing of information, along with humor and laughter, also helps to keep the mood light no matter what the weather or the situation. We've observed, a good guide spends time with each member of the group, not just the most interesting people, and helps everyone feel a special part of the group.

With a lot of money being spent, people have to feel a sense of trust before making a decision to embark on a journey, which could be 'the trip-of-a-lifetime'
Rick and Marilyn Barry, Canada

17. What makes a great guide? Well, being charged by a lioness (with cubs) while you are on foot is pretty exciting and watching 4 lions kill 3 buffaloes in one morning makes for a memorable holiday. These types of experiences tends to form a bond with you and your guide. I will remember those exciting moments and my guide for the rest of my life. However, it is the luck of the draw what can happen on any given day, and it's when there is not a lot of game around that a good guide comes into his own. At these times if your guide is knowledgeable you can learn so much about plants, birds and insects. I have had guides/drivers in Kenya, who stop the vehicle in front of lions and pull out a newspaper to read. The best guide is the one who is enjoying the experience with you and is just as moved and excited as you are. Being with someone whose love and wonder of nature is the same as yours makes for the best sort of guide. I guess that is why they do it and I hope they continue to.
Rey Pearce, Melbourne, Australia

18. What do I need in a guide? What do I want to see in a guide?
1) *Personable, knowledgeable and keen...displaying a passion for the wild.*

First, at the arrival of my group, I very much enjoy a keen, smiling, confident guide. One who greets me as the tour leader (establishing and acknowledging my role), but immediately turning to the group and introducing himself one-on-one to each individual, establishing good eye contact with each during this first interaction.

My group members have spent an incredible amount of their life savings to get here (most of my clients have had to save for the trip, some even borrow). Each one is nervous but excited, and eager with anticipation. In selling this trip to my clients, I have based much of my trip upon the expertise and quality of the guides we will meet along the way. Because of this, I am equally as nervous as the clients when I am utilizing the services of a new guide!

To sell an expensive safari is often a time consuming, sometimes tense and stressful effort. In many cases the final sale is a result of several years of personal discussions with an individual or couple at various social events. Many times the potential client has attended numerous slide shows of mine, has seen or heard several of my radio and television appearances, and, most importantly, has confirmed the quality of my trips from word of mouth discussions with others who have been with me.

Those of whom have never experienced this end of the business simply cannot understand the difficulties involved and the immense personal time investment, let alone the set up costs that the travel company that I work with has incurred. The guides are a critical link to the ultimate success of the trip.

In short, I think the guides displaying passion towards the wild and his method of communication of that passion are what makes or breaks a successful guide. *Passion is the key word.*

This passion is only acquired through a genuine and sincere relationship with the wild, capped with knowledge, curiosity and experience. Well read, articulate methods of communication during the walks or drives need to be done with a sensitivity displaying the understanding that most of the clients on a trip are not necessarily naturalists, and come to the African bush with little real nature experience. These are wide-eyed neophytes for the most part, and will drink in the experience, if the experience is presented in the appropriate manner.

2) *A sense of how to communicate that passion.*

On walks, making sure that the entire walk does not become a rambling monologue of information spewed forth. Rather, setting the mood first of perhaps a quiet, observational meander, where interesting sightings or concepts will be

explained during short stops. Then the exploration continues. The guide should note that Northern Hemisphere clients have a different physiology than that of your heat tolerant one. Care should be taken to do any mini-lectures, no matter how short, in the shade of a bush or tree

Dinner time. This is a time for a certain amount of daily recapping, when the timing is appropriate, to set the minds of the clients both the days experiences, and to get the group anticipating the adventures of tomorrow. Once the safari is long over, I hear from past clients time and again, that some of the most memorable events of a trip, aside from the incredible wildlife viewing, are the real-life stories from the guides.

Clients have a never-ending fascination with the guides. In their mind, guides lead a fairy-tail life. And in reality, they do! The quality locations that guides find themselves working in are some of the best and most profound wildlife landscapes in the world. These places are quickly diminishing:

Fact...in my 44 years of existence on Planet Earth, mankind has eliminated 50% of the remaining forests, and the world population has doubled from 3 to 6 billion.

Our effects on the planet are profound, and will continue to be more so for the foreseeable future. The parks and wild areas of Africa represent some of the best remaining wild areas in the world, complete with storybook animals. People who go to Africa on a quality safari will likely be introduced to a life changing experience, if presented in the appropriate way.

Guides should know when to turn off the vehicle; know how to make the group silent without feeling uneasy (our society is needlessly verbose, and feel uncomfortable in silence); know when enough is said and when to let the experience take over; know their information. These guides make the trip.

3) *Know your clients, and attempt to understand life from their perspective.*

I now take great care in ensuring that my clients are well prepared psychologically for the intensity of parts of the trip, and the incredible privilege it is to be where we are or where we will be going. I also reinforce the fact that the guides are professional and want to give the client the best possible experience possible. I explain that they will do everything they can to be safe, but, if the opportunity presents itself, we will find ourselves in situations where the client may wonder about their safety.

I reinforce in different ways, they must seize the moment, and enjoy the privilege of the incredible knowledge of the guide: he knows how close to go, when to move, and how to behave.

Brian Keating, Head of Conservation Outreach, Calgary Zoological Society.

19. One's enjoyment of a safari depends a great deal on the expertise and congeniality of one's guides. We expected our guides to be knowledgeable about the animals and the environment, to provide the best possible game-viewing opportunities and to ensure that we would feel safe at all times. All of our guides met the first two of these expectations. One of the guides at Chikwenya camp proved capable of safeguarding clients when he was forced to shoot an elephant which charged his walking group, dropping her at their feet.

Pat and Steve Strom, USA

20. For Bettie and me the first few moments at a camp set the stage for our stay. This applies not only to the set up of the camp itself but also to the guides and staff that are there. Obviously the camp must be clean and tidy with well maintained vehicles. We are always impressed with the turn out of the operators/guides and their staff in so far as dress is concerned. Bettie and I have been in camps in Botswana and Ecuador where the gear was terrible, dirty and in disrepair and the guides looked like they

had just climbed out from under a rock. The guide's appearance and bearing on first meeting his guests would be of paramount importance to me. First impressions are lasting impressions.

Our first trip to Africa in 1990 was like all high-end travel: it was very expensive indeed and when you pay that kind of money, you should be able to set your expectations fairly high. We wanted to see animals of every kind and birds and also see the total landscape and generally get the feel of the entire place. We wanted to walk the land, feel the water, smell the trees, touch the earth and let our minds wander to earlier times when Africa was young. We have had that experience from all our trips. However it is the guides enthusiasm with each and every encounter that makes some trips more memorable than others.

Enthusiasm should not end at the dropping of the sun. Rather, spending quiet or down time with the guides has also become a very important part of travel for us. After a long day of walks, game drives and animal watching, it is still very nice to be able to discuss the day's events over supper or during an after-dinner drink. This is indeed a time for guides to get to know their guests even better since during the day most of the talk is about the here and now! When guides show a genuine interest in the lives of their guests, it clearly shows their 'people' side. So our experience has been that guides who try to show off their knowledge with vast numbers of statistics and animal information and never even asking a guest where on the planet he is from, were in fact some of the least effective guides. We like a little bit of environmental and animal information tempered with a vast ability to interact with your guests, this truly makes the best guides.

It goes without saying that safety is of paramount importance when guiding: I know that safety plays an important role in making the guests feel more comfortable; therefore, a short briefing at the start of any stay is important. Some guides can make a safety briefing a fun type event while others just go through the motions. On one of our trips we received a briefing on what to do if the boat sank four days after we set sail!

Our advice to soon-to-be-guides would be that safety needs to be in the guide's head all the time, but must not be displayed to the guests every second of the day. Temper safety with reality but also never compromise safety.

Bettie and I can now see when guides are just going thru the motions and it is not a pleasant experience for the paying customers. I believe that each and every guide should reassess his or her commitment to the guests they lead. And if they find that they believe they are not performing up to their high standards then they should take some time off and recharge. This is also an area that owners/operators should be concerned about because if the guests continue to have inadequate guides then the company will certainly suffer—and if not caught early in the process, it could be too late. It may be that the constant people interaction overwhelms some guides faster than others—they should then either take some time off or find another profession. I can assure you that we will never go into the La Selva Amazon Camp in Ecuador ever again because these guides lacked real people skills—they were very knowledgeable but that is not the only skill needed to be a true guide. We also spent time in the Okavango with a guide in his mid-20s who was a disgrace to the guiding profession. Totally unorganized and unable to help with animal information, this young man had a difficult time keeping the camp staff from a mutiny. This tented camp will never see our faces again. In 1994 when in Namibia we had a young guide. This was a driving type adventure into the desert and up to Etosha where we camped and helped with the kitchen details etc. This guide was one of those few who could do it all. He was well organized be it cooking for the ten of us, fixing a flat tire, setting up or taking down camp or finding great views of animals. Again he had that ability to bring out the best in client/guide relations. He enlightened us on southern African geography, political history, its peoples and their culture and the natural history. He also enjoyed a beer at the end of the day with us and he has remained a very good friend. One final observation from Bettie: she truly appreciates a guide who not only shows us their space but also shares that space with us.

Norm and Bettie Altenhof, Calgary, Canada

21. Guides must communicate constantly. They must also suffer fools, without revealing that they are not doing it gladly. Therefore, a good sense of humour is needed. All of my half a dozen guides ranging from Botswana to Kenya and covering both walking and vehicle safaris have had that most important of attributes in varying degrees, although one of them still allowed himself to be provoked by a client's philosophical argument against the culling of elephants, something which the guide passionately believed was necessary. The periodic bickering cast a shadow

over an otherwise enjoyable time in the bush. My first guide was very knowledgeable, thoroughly enjoyed finding wildlife for us, communicated information about the bush and its inhabitants freely, issued warnings (e.g. about not standing in an open vehicle in the presence of lions) firmly but in a friendly way, was patient and had that sense of humour.

From that point on, that's broadly what I've expected of my guides, and none has let me down. There have been some differences, of course, in communicating information, a couple have relied a little more than the others on clients asking questions. One or two have seemed to be a little less conscious of the needs of photographers. Obviously expert, engendering confidence, tireless, good-humored, obliging, easy-going but firm in the field, a good talker around the campfire, presentable, I think I'd be a bit doubtful about somebody who looked a bit slobby; not that I've had one like that.

John Milbank, ex-journalist, freelance writer/photographer, Adelaide, South Australia

22. We expect a great deal from a safari guide. We expected competence, and received true excellence. We now know that the quality of a safari guide can have a profound impact on our safari experience. At our very first safari camp, we were utterly awed by our guides' ability to identify any of 400 bird species at a mere glance or sound of its call. Since then, our standards have been continually raised by the guides themselves. Were it not for the influence of our safari guides, we might not have been instilled with the passion for natural history and for Africa that we now share. To us, a safari is all about experiencing and photographing wild Africa. Simply stated, we depend on our guides to facilitate our wildlife experience. Knowledge is the key to a guide's effectiveness. When we are on safari, we have no doubt prepared ourselves by reading about the natural history of the area. But a guide can enhance our experience by sharing knowledge that simply cannot be gleaned from a book. This process begins with field identification of wildlife species, both flora and fauna, but it does not end there.

We want to know what makes each species unique: its physical and physiological characteristics, its behaviour patterns and social structures, its interaction with other species, its place in the order of the ecosystem. How is a gemsbok able to survive in such a harsh environment as the Namib Desert? What would happen if there were no dung beetles? How can so many different kinds of eagles thrive in Africa when we in Canada have only two? And we want to understand the interaction between wildlife and the human race: how a species successfully co-exists with mankind or why it does not, and what efforts are underway to protect those species that are threatened by our hand. Is there any hope for the African wild dog, the black rhino or the wattled crane? A good guide will share a profound understanding of the African wilderness, by helping us to fully explore its subtleties and appreciate its intricate web of life. It is a guide's knowledge that gives him something to share about wild Africa, but it is his personality that allows him to make a connection with us. He must be outgoing and articulate, as there is no better tool than effective communication. And he must be flexible, so that he can adapt to the demands of different safari-goers. Some may be content with a no-nonsense, factual dissertation on elephant ecology. We want to know about the guide's personal experiences, insights and opinions. Some tourists seek nothing but the Big Five, equipped with no more than a checklist. We are after a complete African experience, armed with cameras, video recorders, field guides and writing journals. Finally, a guide must demonstrate competence and instill us with a great deal of confidence. Africa can be dangerous and intimidating to the uninitiated. And yet a true appreciation of its beauty can be gained only by an intimate exploration of its landscapes. For us to focus on the wonders of flora and fauna, we must trust that our guide will keep us out of danger. And because nature is unpredictable, we must have confidence that our guide will ably handle any potentially hazardous situation that we might encounter.

We expect a safari guide to be many things. He is at once our host, our field guide, our teacher, our chauffeur, our medic, our navigator, our conservationist, our chaperone, our protector, our counsel, our friend.

We can say with certainty and honesty that our African safari experiences would be much less rich without the contribution of our guides.

Malcolm and Trish Lund, Calgary, Alberta, Canada

23. For my remarks below, I shall be giving my views of the expectations of a visitor to Africa whose dream is to 'go on a safari' to see wildlife and to experience the 'African bush'. My perspective also concerns persons going on a 'photo safari' and not a 'hunting safari'.

First of all, the average US citizen's knowledge about African politics and African wildlife has increased a lot since we planned our first trip to Africa in

1992. Unfortunately, although news about Africa in the media is usually informative, it is also usually about something bad - wars, political instability and corruption, guerrilla activities, natural disasters, ivory and rhino horn poaching, animal species endangerment, and disease - like Ebola or how bad the Aids epidemic is, etc.

The level of knowledge we had in 1992 about Africa was typical. We had only a very rough idea of what the countries were and where they were on the continent. We viewed a "safari" in somewhat mystical terms and initially had visions of what to expect from Hollywood movies. We had seen none of the wildlife documentaries and wildlife videos available today. Our desire to go on safari overrode our concerns about what we knew about political instabilities in the countries to be visited or about exotic diseases we might contract. We expected to see 'animals' but had no idea about the numbers of animals or the varieties of animals we would see. We wanted a "bush experience," but didn't really know what that meant. We knew nothing about either African birds or plants, and probably didn't even think about either before we went. I don't believe we thought specifically about the guiding either. Since we felt that the safari being planned was very expensive, we certainly expected to have competent guides and good treatment. Of course an incompetent guide, or a badly maintained or operating vehicle, or bad food would have kept our high expectations from being realized, but that was not considered before we left for Africa. We did worry about the weather and the climate. We were going to Zimbabwe first and Zimbabwe was having a drought. We also worried about disturbing the ecology or bothering the animals we were to view. Fortunately, we had read Mark Nolting's book, *Africa's Top Wildlife Countries*, and because of that had telephoned Mark for further information.

All of what I have been writing boils down to this: on our first trip our expectations before the safari were concerned with the overall safari experience and not with any specific thought about the guiding. This is because we had no idea of the importance of the guide to the success of the African experience before we got to Africa. We know that now. We had excellent guides and the first trip was a great experience. Their guiding knowledge caused us to want to know more. We have returned every year since. A guide should, first of all, love to be out in the bush himself (or herself). A guide should exhibit an enthusiasm for the ecology and environment and for the preservation of it and a desire to share that enthusiasm. They need to be as knowledgeable as possible about every aspect of the bush, flora and fauna. They need to be as well trained as possible in first aid, and in every situation that might arise in the bush. They should like people. They should be good teachers. Teaching takes place all the time. A guide should also be a good listener and a good learner. He/she should study human nature and try to learn about future clients needs by responding to the needs of the present clients. They should be aware of the total inexperience and lack of knowledge that their clients have about the bush and spend sufficient time in bush safety talks. For example, clients have no knowledge about how near to an animal it is generally safe to be whether in a vehicle or on foot. While the distance chosen by the guide might be safe, the client may not feel comfortable. It is the guide's responsibility to be responsive to the 'comfort level' of the client while at the same time educating the client about the animal and its usual behavioral patterns. Clients must be thoroughly instructed about camp safety, both during the day and the night. Safety talks concerning walking in the bush should also be thorough. The guide should be truthful. If a guide does not know the answer to a question, he/she should say so and not speculate without so informing the clients. While a "fabricated" answer may satisfy the client at the time, later if they learn that the guide was wrong, all guides suffer. It is the guide's responsibility to try to provide excellent guiding to the first timer as well as to someone in the same group who may be returning to Africa after several safaris. A guide should determine as early as possible the experience of the clientele on safaris, who planned the safari, what the client's particular interest in the bush is, etc. If possible, persons with similar knowledge or experience or desires should be placed together on game drives. I believe that most first-timers are most likely to be interested in seeing the "big five" and will have little interest in a certain variety of lark. That does not mean that the lark sighting should be omitted. It is the guide's responsibility to determine how much emphasis should be placed on any sighting of any animal or plant based on the clientele, the available time, and other priorities. Interest in birds is an acquired taste for most people. It should be cultivated, but cultivated carefully. The same is true about the amount of time spent on animal spoor or plants. The wonders of nature should be fed but not force-fed by the guide. Properly maintained, well working, reliable equipment is essential for a successful safari and should be a priority for a guide. Guides should correct any problems as soon as possible. This includes vehicles and camp equipment. Weak batteries or a malfunction when starting a vehicle in the bush will ruin a safari, whether or not any real danger was present at the time. We have been on game drives where each time the driver turned off the vehicle, the clients had to get out and push to get it started. That would be OK if it happened on one time out—equipment can break down, but this was what happened on each game drive for four days. The same is true for tents that don't zip properly or fully, or ants in a sugar bowl at every meal. Camp staff should be friendly, businesslike, and efficient. Guides should not reprimand or discipline staff in the presence of clients.

I conclude with some examples of how we didn't wish guides to behave. The use of radio communication in vehicles can be a sore point. We have been on game drives where the two-way radio is blaring on the whole drive. Besides the effect such sound may have on the game, it also irritates the clients. When game is close in spite of the noise, the audio on video shots is ruined as well as the possible sounds from the animals or environment. Some guides seem to feel that the intelligence gained from learning where the animals are (from the radio) exceeds good game drive practice. Some drivers in certain reserves now have ear plugs, so that the sound is not heard by the clients. This is better, but it affects the quality of the guiding, since the guide spends a good deal of time listening. Guides shouldn't 'push' a confrontation with animals. We have had guides who provoke animals

intentionally (not realizing until we said something) in order for clients to get 'good shots' with cameras. I once wanted to video tape a giraffe walking away from us just ahead of our vehicle. The giraffe was making quite distinct tracks in the road bed. I thought a close-up of a track followed by a pan to the animal making the track would be a good idea. When I asked the guide to stop to enable me to get the shot, he said that he could not understand why anyone would want to photograph the track of an animal. I got the shot anyway, but my opinion of the quality of the guiding dropped considerably. My point here is that the guide should have stopped because I asked him to in spite of not understanding what I was trying to do. It was not worth my time explaining to him the value of recognizing tracks. We had a guide who stated that the only reason that guides stop to talk about some plant species or some practical use or traditional use of a plant or about an insect is because they need to do something to fill the time when there is no game. I hope this is not true. We have been with a guide who worked very hard at making sure that we saw and photographed the 'big five.' Once this had been accomplished, he must have felt that he had done his job, because even though we were with him for several more days after that, he was quite reluctant to take us on any more game drives. He did take us out each day at our urging, but with none of his earlier enthusiasm or friendliness. Overall, we have been very fortunate to have had for the most part excellently trained, wonderful guides. This is true in every African country (south of the Sahara) we have visited (Botswana, Kenya, Namibia, South Africa, Tanzania, Uganda, Zambia and Zimbabwe).
Steve Brady, USA

24. I'm from California, but I've been traveling the African continent for 12 years and crossed 20 African countries thus far. I've been to most of the major national parks, some repeatedly, and I've seen the wide range of technical capabilities and philosophies demonstrated by guides, from country to country, and from guide to guide.

I've been with some of the best on the continent, guides who never look at a clock, walking and tracking with me up to eight hours a day. Guides who are both wise and fearless in their ability to track and orchestrate close encounters on foot, plus are willing to teach me their secret insights. Things like how to closely approach lions on foot, how to survive the charge of a bull Black rhino, how to appease a protective mother elephant or turn a boisterous bull, and the list goes on. Guides who've lived in the bush for 30 years and whom I've seen heroically bite their tongues as an arrogant guest insist that he knows "the correct bird" better than the guide. Guides who know intuitively when to be quiet and just let the clients talk, and when prompted, tell amazing stories. Guides whose vehicle, and meals, and staff are top of the line. And the list goes on.

On the flip side I've met some real characters:

- a guide who as the two of us were tracking lions on foot had his cell phone go off and talked for 10 minutes (it was a friend who wanted to talk about motocycles),
- a guide with six clients on foot, 50 feet from 4 lionesses and one furious male lion, put his rifle down and pushed a client out of the way so he could take pictures,
- a guide who made insulting sexual comments,
- an alchohlic guide who was not only drunk in camp, but make his clients drive for hours with him to search out cheap booze,
- a guide who was completely unscrupulous by trying to grossly overcharge clients for services,
- a guide serving spoiled food, the FIRST night out,
- and the list goes on.

It has all made for a wealth of amazing experiences over the years. And I'll be back in Africa for a couple months of safari again this August.

Judith Cote, California. USA

Appendix A

List of Guide Training Schools

South Africa

Antares
Field Guide Training Centre
P.O. Box 1573, Phalaborwa, 1390, South Africa
Plot 39, Farm Grietjie 6, Phalaborwa, 1390, South Africa
Tel/Fax: +27 15 769 6006
Mobile: +27 83 286 8281
Email: info@antares.co.za
Website: www.antares.co.za

The owner of Antares is Ian Owtram. He has been involved in wildlife conservation for over 13 years in various different areas.

Antares is situated in the Balule North Nature Reserve, 30 kms from Phalaborwa. The reserve is about 2000 hectares in extent and has access to the Olifants River. Antares has traversing rights over a neighbouring reserve where training specific to the "Big 5" and other large species of game, is carried out. Antares runs a number of courses throughout the year. The courses are run over a six-week period, starting on a Monday and finishing on a Friday. The course follows the syllabus set out by The Field Guides Association of Southern Africa (FGASA). The subjects covered are diverse and include astronomy, geology, anything to do with fauna and flora, firearm training and levels 1 and 2 first aid courses.

EcoTraining
Cnr Ehmke and Van der Merve, Outpost Centre,
Jock and Java, Nelspruit, South Africa
PO Box 19122, Nelspruit, 1200, South Africa
Tel: +27 13 752 2536   Fax: +27 13 752 4753
E-mail: enquiries@ecotraining.co.za
Website: www.ecotraining.co.za

Damelin College in Johannesburg offers a 2-year, full-time, advanced Game Ranging Course, including Eco Training (part of FGASA) (tel. +2711 440 7020).

EcoTraining was established in 1993 to provide potential nature guides with the basic grounding, knowledge and professionalism required to enter this rapidly-growing industry. Since then, hundreds of students have attended their courses and many of them have gone on to establish successful careers in the eco-tourism business. EcoTraining's camp is situated in the northern Sabi Sand Game Reserve, part of the greater Kruger National Park ecosystem, which is famous for its abundance of wildlife. EcoTraining is owned by two highly experienced guides, Lex Hes and Anton Lategan. Lex brings more than 20 years of guiding experience into the business and is also a successful wildlife photographer and author. Anton has worked as a guide in some of southern Africa's top game lodges and has travelled widely throughout southern Africa, visiting most of the remote wilderness areas in the region.

Together, Lex and Anton have designed training courses which are carried out by a dynamic and dedicated team of professional trainers, all experienced in their fields.

Basic Course Outline

Day 1: Introduction to ecotourism and guiding, field guiding as a profession; personal attributes of a field guide; guiding skills and duties. Day 2: Bush navigation and orientation; basic ecology; geology; soil-types; weather and plant communities. Day 3: Basics of plant identification and plant uses; presentation skills. Day 4: Animal tracks and tracking. Day 5: Basics of bird identification. Day 6: Basic animal behaviour; approaching dangerous game. Day 7: Setting up a basic bush camp; basic bush and survival skills. Day 8: Dangerous game rifles; the game drive vehicle; night drives and the use of a spotlight; basic 4x4 driving skills. Day 9: Planning of game drives and walks; radio procedures. Day 10: Reptiles and amphibians; sensitivity. Day 11: Anticipating animal behaviour; astronomy. Day 12: Invertebrates. Day 13: Mid-course exam. Day 14: Day of leisure. Day 15: Basic habitat management. Day 16: The 12 S's; photography and use of binoculars. Day 17: Communication and facilitation skills. Day 18: Shooting exercises. Day 19: Dealing with guests. Day 20: Manyeleti/KNP border visit, conservation and anti-poaching. Day 21: Freshwater fish and Africam. Day 22: Sustainable development and the wise use of natural resources. Day 23: Ecotourism and the local communities. Day 24: Solitaire; taxonomy. Day 25: Working in the industry. Day 26: Final exam. Day 27: Game drive assessments. Day 28: Departure.

Botswana

Eco-tourism Support Services
Peter Hancock
P.O. Box 20463, Maun, Botswana
Tel/Fax: +267 662 481
E-mail: pete@info.bw

Eco-tourism Support Services offers a basic guides course comprising guest and public relations, laws governing the safari industry, natural history, tourism, field skills, campcraft, guided safaris, and environmental studies, conservation issues, geography of the country, photography, etc. This course can be run as a complete short public course or separately to safari companies who require tailor-made courses. A modified version of the course is also offered to mokoro polers.
The course is accredited by the Hotel and Tourism Association of Botswana (HATAB).

Regional Tourism Associations

Botswana
HATAB
Hospitality and Tourism Association of Botswana
Private Bag 00423, Gaborone, Botswana
Tel: +267 395 7144 / 395 6898
Fax: +267 390 3201
E-mail: hatab@hatab.bw
Website: www.hatab.bw

Kenya
KPSGA
Kenya Professional Safari Guides Association
P.O. Box 24397, 00502, Nairobi, Kenya
Tel: +254 20 609 355 / 577 018
Fax: +254 20 609 355 / 604 730
Mobile: +254 721 448 428
E-mail: info@safariguides.org
Website: www.safariguides.org

Namibia
TASA
Tour and Safari Association of Namibia
P.O Box 11534, Windhoek, Namibia
Tel: +264 61 238 423
Fax: +264 61 238 424
E-mail: info@tasa.na
Website: www.tasa.na

South Africa
FGASA
The Field Guides Association of Southern Africa
P.O. Box 4432, Cresta, 2118, South Africa
Tel: +27 11 886 8245
Fax: +27 11 886 8084
E-mail: education@fgasa.org.za
Website: www.fgasa.org.za

Zimbabwe
SOAZ
Safari Operators Association of Zimbabwe
18 Walter Hill Avenue, Eastlea, Harare, Zimbabwe
Tel: +263 4 702 402
Fax +263 4 705 046
E-mail: soaz@mweb.co.zw
Website: www.soaz.net

Appendix B

Recommended Reading for Guides

Allan, David; **Photographic Guide to the Birds of Prey of Southern, Central & East Africa;** Soft cover; Struik; Cape Town.

Bechky, Allan; **Adventuring in East Africa;** Sierra Club Books; San Francisco.

Bechky, Allan; **Adventuring in Southern Africa;** Sierra Club Books; San Francisco.

Branch, **Field Guide to the Snakes and other Reptiles of Southern Africa;** Soft cover; Struik; Cape Town.

Bosman & Hall-Martin; **Cats of Africa;** Fernwood Press; Cape Town.

Bothma, J; **Larger Carnivores of Southern Africa;** Van Schaik; Cape Town.

Carnaby, Trevor; **Beat about The Bush;** Jacana Media; Johannesburg.

Carruthers, Vincent; **Frogs and Frogging in Southern Africa;** Soft cover; Struik; Cape Town.

Carruthers, Vincent, edited by; **The Wildlife of Southern Africa** - A Field Guide to the Animals and Plants of the region; Soft cover; Struik; Cape Town.

Coates Palgrave; **Trees of Southern Africa;** Struik; Cape Town.

Estes, Richard; **Safari Companion** - A Guide to Watching African Mammals; Soft cover; Russel Friedman Books; Johannesburg.

Fitzgerald; **Stars of the Southern Skies;** Soft cover; Witwatersrand University press; Johannesburg.

Funston, Paul; **Bushveld Trees;** Fernwood Press; Cape Town.

Kemp, A; **Sasol Birds of Prey of Africa;** Struik; Cape Town.

Kingdon, Jonathan; **The Kingdon Guide to African Mammals;** Natural World Academic Press; USA and UK.

Leroy, Astrid & John; **Spiderwatch in Southern Africa;** Soft cover; Struik; Cape Town.

Liebenberg, Louis; **The Art of Tracking;** Soft cover; David Philip; Cape Town.

MacLean; **Roberts Birds of South Africa;** Hardcover; Voelcker Bird Book Fund; Cape Town.

Moss, Cynthia; **Elephant Memories** - Thirteen Years in the Life of an Elephant Family; Elm Tree Books; London.

Moss, Cynthia; **Portraits of the Wild** - Animal Behavior in East Africa; University of Chicago Press; USA.

Newman, Kenneth; **Newman's Birds of Southern Africa;** PVC Field Edition; Struik; Cape Town.

Nolting, Mark W; **Africa's Top Wildlife Countries;** Global Travel Publishers Inc.; USA.

Payne, Katy; **Silent Thunder** - The Hidden Voices of Elephants; Jonathan Ball Publishers; UK.

Reay Smithers; **Mammals of Southern Africa**

Roodt, Veronica; **Common Wild Flowers of the Okavango;** The Shell Field Guide Series; Shell Oil; Botswana.

Roodt, Veronica; **Trees and Shrubs of the Okavango Delta;** The Shell Field Guide Series; Shell Oil; Botswana.

Skaiffe, SH & Ledger; **African Insect Life;** Struik; Cape Town.

Smit; **Guide to the Acacias of South Africa;** Briza; Pretoria.

Stuart, C & T; **Field Guide to the Mammals of Southern Africa;** Soft cover; Struik; Cape Town.

Stuart, C & T; **Field Guide to Tracks & Signs of Southern and East African Wildlife;** Soft cover; Struik; Cape Town.

Tarboton, Warwick; **Guide to the Nests and Eggs of Southern African Birds;** Struik; Cape Town.

Van Oudtshoorn; **Guide to the Grasses of Southern Africa;** Briza; Pretoria.

Van Wyk; **Field Guide to the Trees of Southern Africa;** Soft cover; Struik; Cape Town.

Index

About the Author

Garth Thompson was born and raised in Zimbabwe. His three children are fifth-generation Zimbabweans. He has played a prominent role in the region's tourist trade for the past 26 years, being one of the pioneers of Zimbabwe's fledgling tourism industry since its independence in 1980. Starting out as a wildlife guide at the age of 21 in Hwange National Park, he went on to own and operate safari operations in Mana Pools National Park in the Zambezi Valley. During this time, assisted by his wife Mel, they opened a tour operation, aimed initially at marketing and booking their safaris. This company went on to become a prominent supplier of guests to many camps and lodges in Zimbabwe and its neighbouring countries. He was nominated as the Tourism Personality of 1988.

Garth has guided in most parks in Zimbabwe, Botswana, Tanzania, Kenya and Namibia and to a lesser extent in Rwanda, Uganda, Mocambique and Zambia. His favorite safaris are on foot and by canoe in the Zambezi Valley, which is where he conducts the majority of his safaris. He enjoys a following of long standing clients, who safari with him on a regular basis. Most have become lifelong friends.

For any additional information and ideas you may have on guiding he welcomes contact at e-mail address: gartht@mweb.co.zw

Other titles by Jacana Media:

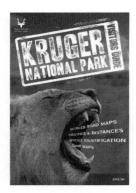

*Kruger National Park
Visitors Guide*; also available in
Afrikaans, French and German

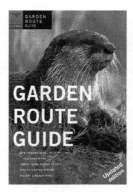

Garden Route Guide

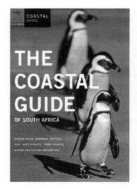

*The Coastal Guide
of South Africa*

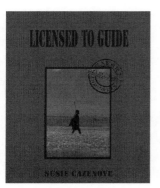

Licensed to Guide

Wildcare

*Masai Mara
Visitor Map Guide*

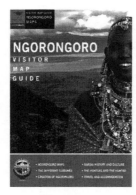

*Ngorongoro
Visitor Map Guide*

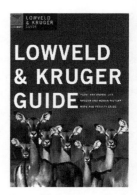

Lowveld & Kruger Guide

Roberts Bird Guide
South Africa; also
available in Afrikaans

Roberts Bird Guide
Kruger National Park;
also available in Afrikaans

A Landscape of Insects
and other Invertebrates

Beat about the Bush
– Mammals

Beat about the Bush
– Birds

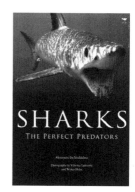

Sharks
The Perfect Predators

A Delight of Owls

Insider's Guide

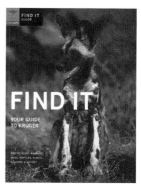

Find It
Your Guide to Kruger;
also available in Afrikaans
and German

See a complete list of Jacana titles at www.jacana.co.za

Notes

Notes

Notes